# Stained Glass
## *Painting*

# Stained Glass
## *Painting*

Julie Lafaille

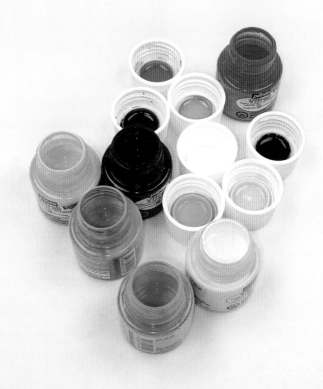

STACKPOLE
BOOKS

Copyright 2015 by Stackpole Books
Copyright Ottawa 2013 Broquet Inc.
Originally published in 2013 by Broquet Inc. (French language)

Published by
STACKPOLE BOOKS
5067 Ritter Road
Mechanicsburg, PA 17055
www.stackpolebooks.com

Printed in the United States of America

10 9 8 7 6 5 4 3 2 1

First edition

ISBN 978-0-8117-1419-8

Cataloging-in-Publication Data is on file with the Library of Congress.

Text, photos, and patterns copyright Julie Lafaille
Editing: Andrée Laprise
Proofreading: Lise Roy
Page design/layout: Anabelle Gauthier
Translation: Kathryn Fulton

The author and editors of this work cannot be held responsible for the results obtained by using the information in this book, which is given in good faith.

# Contents

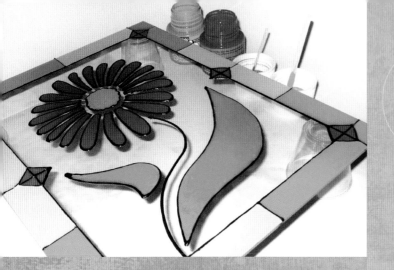

# Foreword

**A book full of ideas!**

This book is the result of long years devoted almost entirely to the art of stained glass painting. What a pleasure it was to test all the products and mediums in order to select the best ones. What a pleasure it was as well to invent spectacular and original effects. Although there are many possibilities when it comes to faux stained glass, in this book I've brought together the most useful and clear information that I've accumulated over these last years. Here, then, is the result of my searching, a wide array of tricks and tips on the subject.

I hope you have as much fun making the projects in this book as I had creating them. You will quickly see that the world of stained glass painting is fabulous and full of possibilities.

Have fun!

*Julie Lafaille*

Julie Lafaille
www.juliescraftingideas.com
julielafaille@juliescraftingideas.com

I would like to thank the following people, without whom this book would never have come to be: Bruno Bérubé, Élisabeth and Myriam Bérubé, Lucie Lapointe and Normand Lafaille, and Antoine Broquet.

# Introduction

Stained glass painting is a technique for painting on glass to simulate the look of leaded or soldered stained glass. You don't have to cut or assemble pieces of glass here, because everything is painted directly on the glass. Furthermore, the materials needed are simple and affordable, making it a very accessible hobby for anyone who wants to give it a try.

This book contains all the information you need to make a piece of basic faux stained glass (on a glass surface), but you will also find many projects for working on less-common surfaces, such as a mirror, a sheet of acetate, even a block of wood—it's all about stimulating the imagination.

Although it's tempting to read just the chapter you're interested in, it's better to read the whole book, in order, the first time, in order to understand the process well. Certain information and techniques are explained fully only in the chapters that concern them and are only summarized in the project chapters that follow.

Finally, the many projects in this book are all different, to allow you to practice the techniques but also to show you diverse possibilities. Don't hesitate to change the size or colors of any of the projects and adapt the patterns to use on different surfaces, according to your taste and your decor.

With stained glass painting, *anything* is possible with a little imagination!

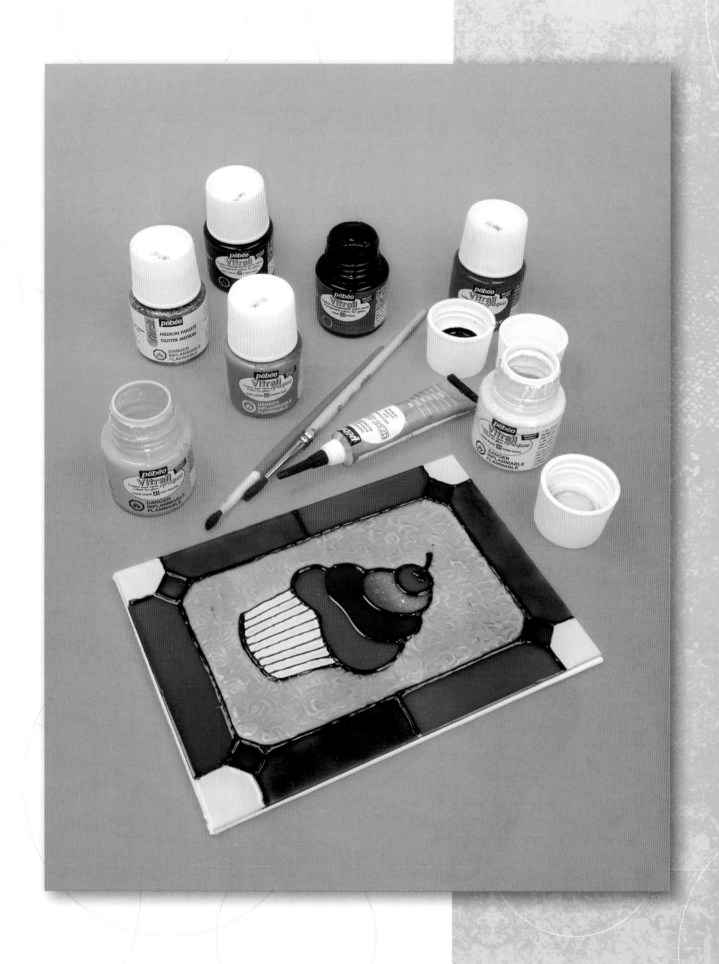

# Chapter 1

# Products, tools, and surfaces

All the products, tools, and surfaces you need to do stained glass painting.

# *Products*

Here are the principal products needed for stained glass painting.

## Glass paint

The paints and various mediums used in this book are all from Pebeo's Vitrail line. Other brands, such as DecoArt, Plaid, Delta, and Gallery, have lines of glass paints, too, and they will work just as well. These lines include varieties of transparent, opaque, and metallic colors, which can be mixed to create wonderful new colors. Glass paints are usually solvent based. Before starting to paint, it is important to gently mix the paint in each container with a craft stick to obtain a uniform color.

**Caution:** Do not shake the bottle, or you will end up with lots of little bubbles in the paint.

## Lightening medium

Very useful for lightening colors, this medium can also be used as a varnish or to achieve some surprising special effects. Very shiny finish. Solvent based.

## Glitter medium

This medium adds sparkle to colors. It can also create some interesting effects. Less shiny finish than lightening medium. Solvent based.

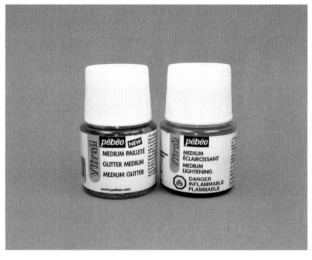

## Drawing the outlines

**Relief outliner:** This paint allows you to rapidly outline a design with many details. You can vary the thickness of the lines by how firmly you squeeze the tube. Water based and available in different colors.

**Adhesive lead strip:** Adhesive lead strip is used for imitating the lead cames in real stained glass projects (which tarnish over time) and works best for straight lines and simple designs.

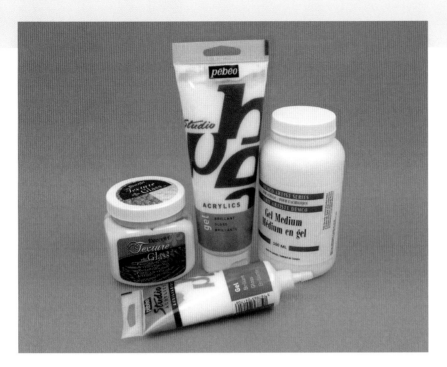

## Acrylic gel medium

Acrylic gel medium allows you to create textures on glass. It goes on white but dries clear. The thick, creamy texture offers a multitude of possibilities. Available in many varieties and brands (check to make sure the brand you choose dries clear; some gel mediums have a matte finish). Tools used with gel medium can be cleaned with water.

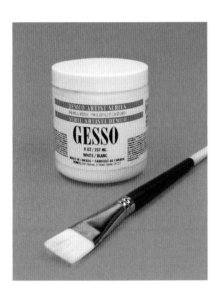

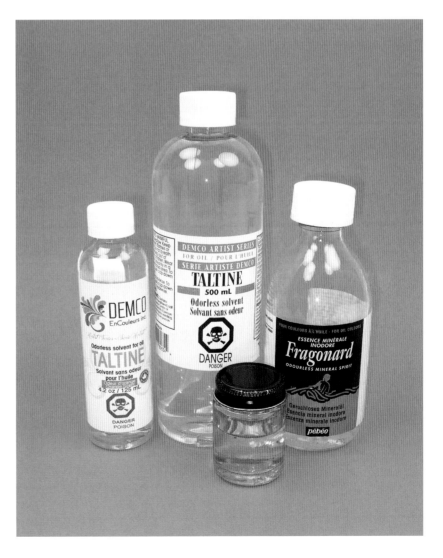

## White gesso

On an opaque surface, white gesso can be used as a background to yield brighter colors. Apply it using a flat paintbrush with synthetic bristles; clean the brush with water.

## Solvent

Solvent (or mineral spirits) is indispensable for cleaning brushes used with glass paints and mediums. Available in odorless or citrus-scented varieties; use whichever you prefer.

# Tools

**Here are the principal tools you need for stained glass painting.**

## Toothpicks

Regular and larger, flattened "club-sandwich-style" toothpicks allow you to paint small sections of a project. Avoid the round, very pointy toothpicks because they are less effective at spreading paint.

## Cotton swabs

Cotton swabs are fantastic for wiping up excess paint and adding drops of paint on top of another color. Look for ones with the cotton ends wrapped tightly around the stick.

## Craft sticks

Craft or popsicle sticks can be used for stirring paint and mixtures created specifically for a particular project.

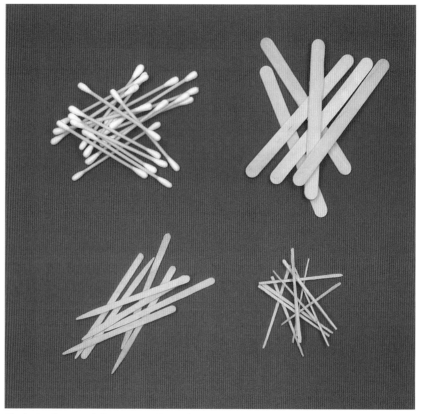

Clockwise from top left: cotton swabs, craft sticks, regular toothpicks, "club-sandwich-style" toothpicks

**Stamps, foam sponges, palette knife, plastic knife, and so on**
These useful little tools can be used to create all kinds of texture effects with gel medium. Other tools are mentioned in the chapter on textures.

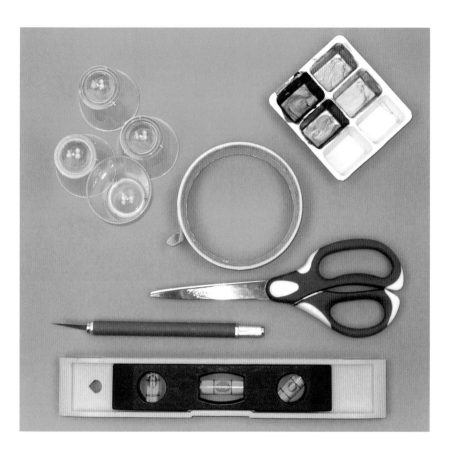

### Masking tape or Scotch tape

Used to attach the pattern on or under the painting surface.

### Small plastic cups

Used to hold glass up off your work surface while applying paint (other objects will work as well).

### Scissors

Used to cut patterns, sponges, lead strips, and more.

### Craft knife

Allows you to trim off excess dry relief outliner or lead strips.

### Level

Essential tool for making sure a piece is level, since the paint is very runny.

### Assorted small containers

For mixing colors.

### Lead pencil

Used to trace additional lines that are not on the pattern.

### Paintbrushes

All kinds of paintbrushes can be used to create different effects with the paint. For painting backgrounds, use natural-bristle brushes, because these bristles are supple and absorbent, allowing you to fill in a section more quickly. In stained glass painting, you usually do not need many brushes. It all depends on the size of the sections that you have to paint. In general, paintbrushes in three different sizes are recommended: small, medium, and large.

### Carbon paper and stylus

You will need black carbon paper and a stylus to copy a design onto an opaque or three-dimensional surface. The stylus can also be used to make small decorative dots on a project.

# Surfaces

**Many surfaces can be used for stained glass painting: glass, plexiglass, acetate, rigid plastic, wood, metal, mirror, canvas, ceramic tile, and more. Although painting on a traditional sheet of glass is great, it is also fun to paint on unique surfaces, such as a thick block of glass, a mirror, or a decorative plaque. Here are some ideas for some surfaces you can use for your projects.**

### Blocks of glass in different thicknesses

Some blocks have a hole in one side that allows you to insert a light.

### Ready-to-paint framed glass

These are great because you can paint or stain the frame to match the glass.

### Decorative wooden plaques

Many sizes and shapes are available. You can also paint on other kinds of wooden pieces, such as boxes, cases, benches, and so on.

### Plexiglass, acetate, and ceramic tile

Sheets of plexiglass come in different thickness and are usually cut to the desired size at the store. You can also use photo frames without the cardboard backs. Note that a sheet of plexiglass can be drilled at the top so it can be hung without a frame.

### Artist's canvas

Pre-stretched canvas can be purchased in many different sizes and thicknesses. For best results, it's best to choose good-quality, tightly stretched canvases.

### Mirror

Painting on a mirror creates wonderful effect. Take care, however, not to scratch the surface as you work on the project, which will leave lasting marks.

# Preparing the surface

# Preparing the surface

**The first step in stained glass painting is to prepare the surface you want to use. Whether you are painting on a mirror, canvas, or a piece of wood, it is very important to do careful prep work so that the paint adheres well when you apply it. Here, then, is how to prepare these surfaces.**

### Glass, mirror, porcelain, ceramic tile
Simply clean the surface with rubbing alcohol and a paper towel to remove all traces of dust and oil.

### Plexiglass, acetate, plastic
Wipe the surface with a clean cloth or a paper towel to remove any dust. (If the plexiglass is covered with a protective sheet, don't forget to remove it.)

### Wood
First, make sure the piece is well sanded and has no rough spots.

If the wood is dark, apply a coat of white gesso on the sections you are going to paint. Make sure the layer of gesso is opaque and covers the grain of the wood (add a second coat if needed). This white base will make the colors applied over it show up clear and bright. Without the gesso, the grain of the wood would be visible, which can be problematic in certain compositions. You can apply gesso only where the design will be if you don't want to paint the whole piece. In this case, transfer the design onto the piece before applying the gesso.

Once the gesso is dry, apply a coat of all-purpose sealant or acrylic varnish to make sure the wood will not absorb the paint once it is applied (especially if there are knots in the wood). This step is not necessary, but it is strongly recommended if you want to obtain a shiny and uniform surface without having to apply many coats of paint.

If the wood is pale and the grain is not very visible, simply apply a layer of

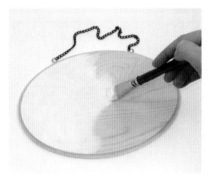

all-purpose sealant or acrylic varnish on the surface to seal it well. This will likely prevent the pattern of the wood from being visible through the colors.

### Canvas
The canvases sold in art and craft stores are generally ready to be painted, so they don't need to be prepared in any way. However, you should know that the texture of the canvas will be visible under the colors, and the surface will absorb the paint a bit. The result will be a painting that is less bright. If you do not want the colors to be absorbed into the canvas, apply a coat of white gesso over the whole surface to seal it. But this step is optional and depends on the result you want.

### Metal
First, clean the surface with a paper towel and rubbing alcohol to remove all traces of dust and oil. The next steps depend on the result you want to obtain and the color (dark or light) of the metal.

If the metal is light, you can paint directly on it. Don't forget, however, that certain light colors, such as yellow, will look slightly different when applied to a metal surface.

If the metal is dark, apply an opaque coat of gesso to make sure the paint colors will show up brightly. You can apply the gesso only to the section where the design will be painted if you don't want to paint the entire piece (again, transfer the design to the piece before applying the gesso). Or you can paint directly on the metal; the colors against the dark background will create a rich and interesting result, even though the colors themselves will look very different.

Close-up of stained glass painting on canvas with the texture visible

# Chapter 3

# Positioning and transferring the pattern

# Positioning and transferring the pattern

**Once the piece is prepared, you need to decide where you want the design to be and transfer the outline to the surface. Again, the method you use depends on the kind of surface you have. See the appropriate instructions below.**

### Flat glass, plexiglass, acetate, transparent plastic

Place the pattern underneath the flat, clear surface and attach it in place with tape. It is important here not to place tape over any lines that must be transferred. Make sure the piece does not stick to the table and can be freely moved in any direction.

### Mirror, canvas, metal, ceramic, three-dimensional pieces (blocks of glass, porcelain objects)

For opaque or three-dimensional surfaces, you'll need to use black carbon paper. First, attach the pattern to the surface with tape (along the top edge only). Next, insert a sheet of carbon paper underneath the pattern—dark side down—and trace along the lines of the pattern with a stylus. Before removing the pattern, check to make sure all the details were transferred, as it is very difficult to put the pattern back in exactly the same place. Any unwanted marks can be removed with an eraser, and a regular lead pencil can be used to fill in small gaps as needed.

> For the patterns in this book, you do not need to trace any dotted lines or the outline of the designs, unless otherwise indicated.

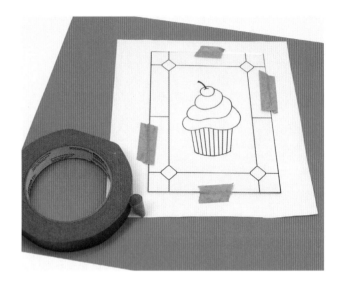

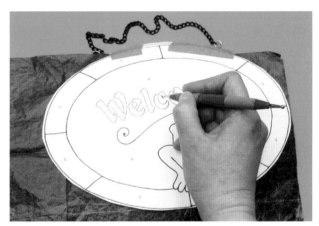

Design transferred to a block of glass

Transferring a design onto wood

<table>
<tr><td>Chapter<br>4</td><td># Outlining<br># the colors</td></tr>
</table>

- **Techniques for using relief outliner**

- **Techniques for using adhesive lead strip**

# Outlining the colors

Once your surface is well prepared and the pattern is transferred, you can start to outline your design using the method of your choice: using a relief outliner or adhesive lead strips. Both techniques are explained in this chapter, so you can choose whichever works best for you (or you can use a combination of the two on the same project if you want). Once you've finished outlining your design, go to the next chapter.

## 1. Techniques for using relief outliner

**Water-based product**
**Drying time: about 30 minutes**

### Preparing the tube

If the tube of relief outliner is new, unscrew the applicator and break the protective seal over the end with the cap or nail (note that the hole created by a thin needle will probably be too small). Screw the applicator back on very tightly. You do not need to cut off the end of the applicator, unless you want to create very thick lines. It can be helpful to warm the tube up between your hands so that the paint will be easier to work with.

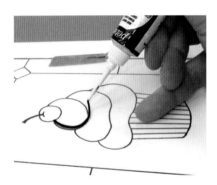
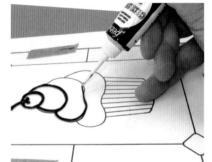
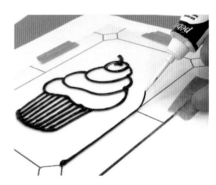

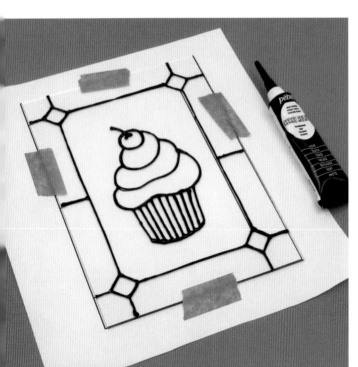

### Apply the outliner

*If you are not familiar with this technique, practice on another surface before outlining the final piece.*

The idea is to "drop" a line of outliner on top of all the lines in the design, keeping the applicator tip just above the surface but not touching it (it's kind of like decorating a cake). It's best to start with the lines in the middle and work gradually toward the outside so you don't run into the already outlined lines. To get an even line, you must maintain a constant pressure on the tube and move slowly. The thickness of the line is important. The thicker the line, the better it will contain the color; the lines shouldn't be irregular or too thin. Make sure each spot where the lines meet is completely closed so the glass paint won't run out in between the lines.

Once the outlines are complete, let the material dry for at least 30 minutes before moving on to the next step. The relief lines should be hard and dry to the touch.

## Making a straight line
### Trick 1
To make a straight, even line, do not drag the tip of the applicator along the surface. Hold it a little ways above the surface and keep it moving while squeezing the tube. The idea is for the line to lie out along the surface uniformly.

### Trick 2
If the first trick doesn't work because your hand is unsteady, you can make a support. To do this, use a ruler, yardstick, or dowel (whatever object you use should be rigid and smooth) that is longer than the longest side of the surface you are working on. Attach two small objects of the same size (I used dice) to the ends of the support to hold it above the surface (A).

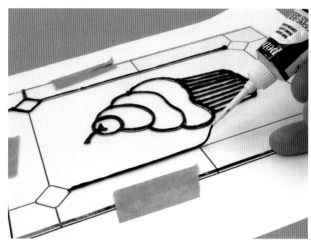
Hold the tip a little ways above the surface

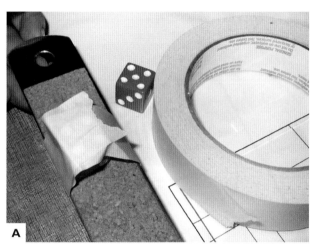
**A** Prepare a support

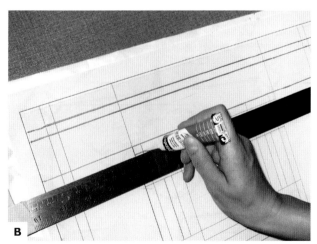
**B** Make the line, resting the top of the tube lightly on the support

Place the support in position over the project so the feet are beyond the edge of the surface. The support must be stable. If it slides a little when you rest your hand on it, place a bit of nonslip mat or a loop of tape under the feet.

Start to make the first line, resting the tube lightly on the support. The applicator tip should be very near the surface but not touching it. Maintain a constant pressure on the tube while moving your hand along the support (B). Practice a bit on another surface to get a feel for the motion and pressure needed. I recommend you do all the horizontal lines in the design first then turn the surface and do the vertical lines.

This support technique doesn't work for everyone but it might be a perfect solution to the challenge of drawing long straight lines.

## Making circles
To create an even circle, first do half, then turn the project around completely and do the other half.

Completed design on canvas

## Correcting mistakes

**For all surfaces:** You can remove excess relief outliner from the surface with a cotton swab immediately after it is applied (A). You can also add a new line over a line that is too thin, for example, to improve it.

**On glass, porcelain, or ceramic:** For these surfaces, there is another possibility—wait until the paint is completely dry and trim off any excess or mistakes with a craft knife (B). This technique is very effective, as it allows you to cleanly and precisely remove any imperfections. You can even slide the blade of the craft knife underneath a line to remove the entire line, if needed (C). Note that this technique doesn't work very well on other surfaces, as the knife can damage them.

## Storing the outliner

Clean the applicator with warm water as soon as you're finished outlining, then dry it. Place a small piece of plastic wrap over the open end of the tube, then put the applicator cap back on. Note that relief outliner keeps best when there is a good amount left in the tube.

### When to use outliner

You can use this product on all kinds of surfaces and for projects with lots of details. It is easy to control and allows you to make thin lines as well as thick ones by varying the pressure you put on the tube. Outliner is available in several colors, so you can match it to your decor. Although the metallic colors are pretty, black is definitely my first choice for several reasons: First, the spots where one line meets another are less visible. Also, painting the sections of the design goes much quicker, as overflow onto the lines doesn't need to be cleaned up. And finally, a stained glass painting made with black relief outliner is beautiful from both sides, which is very useful when you want to hang a piece between two rooms. This is not the case with the lighter colors of relief outliner, such as gold or vermeil gold.

**Disadvantages:** Long straight lines and curves demand extra care and patience. The tubes quickly become fragile and can break if folded multiple times. You have to constantly squeeze the paint down toward the tip of the tube (as with a tube of toothpaste) to avoid air bubbles. A large project with many details requires the purchase of several tubes.

A

B

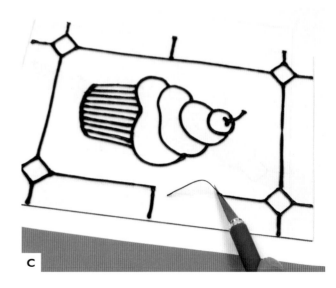

C

## 2. Techniques for using adhesive lead strip

### Double roll

### Preparation

Adhesive lead strip comes ready to use. However, it's best to not use the first layer of lead strip on the roll as it is usually sticky on top.

### Application

Lead strip usually comes in double strips. Start by removing the paper backing that protects the sticky side of the strip. Cut the two halves of the strip apart at the top and use scissors or your fingers to separate the strip, working with a short length at a time (the more you handle the strip, the less well it will stick). You will alternate between halves of the strips to cover the lines of the drawing.

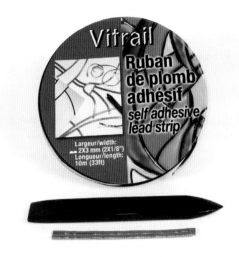

Start with the shortest lines in the design. With one of the strands of lead strip, measure the exact length you need and cut it off with scissors or a craft knife (A).

Place the strip where you want it, pressing enough that it'll stay in place (you can do this with several segments before moving on to the next step).

Using the flat side of a plastic "fid" (the tool that usually comes with the roll), gently press along the length of the strip in order to attach it firmly to the surface (B). The surface of the strip should be smooth. Put extra pressure on the ends of the strip so they won't lift up.

Note that you can use the tip of the plastic tool to move a strip, if necessary.

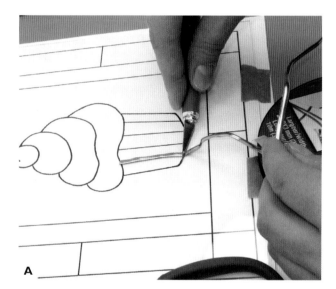

A

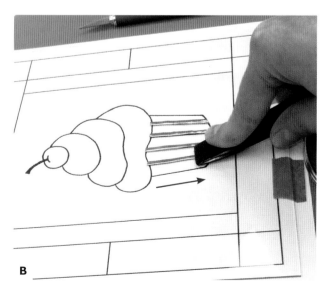

B

C

Proceed in the same way for all the lines of the design, laying them down one by one, overlapping the ends and taking care to press down the overlaps. Remember: sealing these junctions is very important, since the smallest opening will allow the paint to flow out. Don't move too quickly. You can check whether your joints are well sealed by looking at the back side of your piece.

Once all the strips are in place, go on to the next step. Wash your hands with soapy water once you have finished the project.

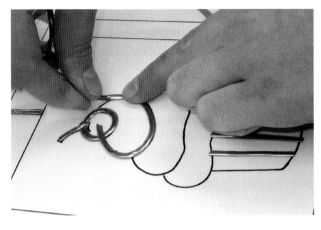

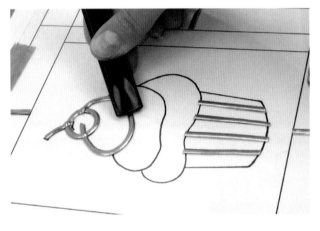

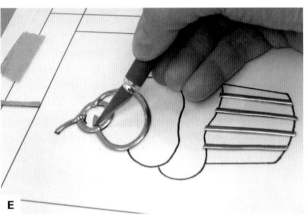

E

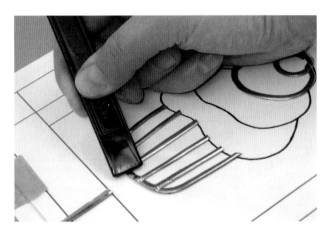

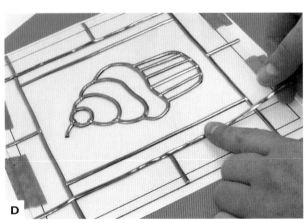

D

STAINED GLASS PAINTING

## Which lines should I start with?

This depends on the design you've chosen. You need to look at which lines overlap to know which ones to place first. In general, it's often best to start with the shorter lines; these are often the ones that go over other lines. But your design may be different. One thing is certain, though—the lines that go all the way across the design (vertically or horizontally) are usually best left for last.

## Hints and tricks

Trim off any excess lead strip with a craft knife directly on the surface (E). This is the most precise technique and gives the best finished result. If it's necessary, it is possible to pull up the strip and reposition it. Also, if the strip is difficult to shape around curves, warm it with a hair dryer. Then use the pointed end of the plastic tool to pull it up and reshape it as needed.

## How do I get the adhesive off the glass?

If you press the lead strip onto the glass and then remove it several times, it is possible that the surface of the glass will get sticky. To remove the adhesive residue, dip a cotton swab in rubbing alcohol and wipe the residue away.

## Storing lead strip

Store the lead strip in an airtight container; otherwise, the metal will become oxidized over time.

## When to use lead strip

Lead strip must be used on rigid surfaces, since it needs to be pressed down in order to get a tight seal. It simulates the lead of a real stained glass window well, as it quickly loses its metallic finish and becomes dull and dark. It is very easy to make straight lines with this product. But it is best to use it for simple designs and projects that will not be visible from the back (for example, a stained-glass window in a cupboard or jewelry box).

**Disadvantages:** Lead strip is more difficult to apply than relief outliner.

It is quite easy to accidentally stain the lead strip when applying the colors. For this reason, you have to constantly wipe off the outlines before the excess paint dries.

The back of a stained-glass painting that uses lead strips isn't very attractive because you can see all the cut ends as well as any color that bled into the junctions. You can fix this problem by placing lead strip over all the lines on the back side, of course, but that is a good deal of extra work.

Back view

Pressing down all the lead strips requires a bit of strength. A design with lots of details can take a long time to complete.

The look of the oxidized lead strips doesn't appeal to everyone. If you don't want the oxidized look, you can use a small paintbrush to apply a thin coat of gloss gel medium over all the lines of lead to seal them. The shiny finish will disappear but the lines will stay solid and dark.

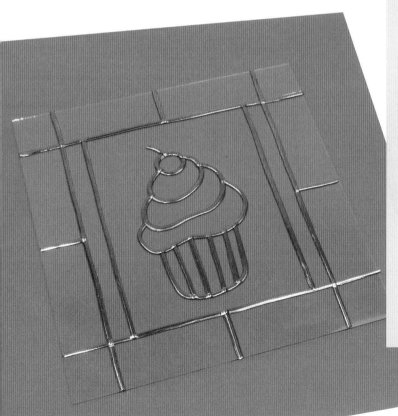

Close-up of textures (central section) p. 80.

# Textures

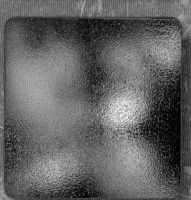

*Note: Creating textures is a personal choice. If you don't want to add texture effects to your project, simply move on to the next chapter.*

# Introduction to textures

Having carefully prepared your surface, transferred your pattern, and outlined the design, you have the option to add textures to certain sections of your project to give them an extra dimension. Doing so is not necessary, of course, and depends entirely on the final look you want. A variety of textures are used in the projects presented in this book.

Adding texture to a stained glass painting greatly enriches the project and gives it a lot of depth. It is also a simple, inexpensive way to simulate the textures of real stained glass. Although acrylic gel medium wasn't originally designed for this use, it is an excellent product to use in stained glass painting.

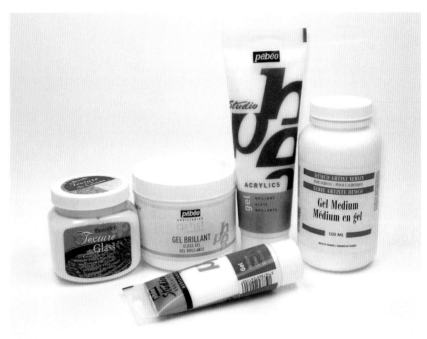

Some of the gel mediums on the market

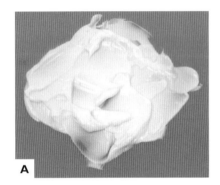

**A**

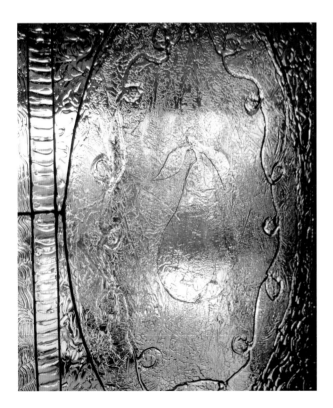

Its creamy, thick consistency, along with its transparency, allows you to create some very surprising effects.

All the textures in this chapter are made using gloss gel medium. Generally sold in tubes or jars, in small or large amounts, and under many brand names, this product is thick, creamy, and smooth (A). It goes on white, becoming completely transparent when it dries. Make sure the product you choose dries clear; certain kinds of gel medium not labeled "gloss" have a more matte finish.

### Types of surfaces

The textures illustrated in this book look nicest and show up best on shiny surfaces such as glass, plexiglass, or a mirror. It *is* possible to add texture to other kinds of surfaces (canvas, wood, metal), but the texture will be less visible on these surfaces, since light doesn't pass through them. For glass and plexiglass, you can even add textures on the back of the project if you wish.

Remember that you can always overlap and combine textures in order to obtain new effects (let the medium dry completely in between applications).

## Working with gel medium

**Applying the product:** To help you see the effects created as you work with gel medium, slide a piece of dark-colored paper underneath the project.

**Tools for working with gel medium:** plastic palette knife, squares of foam sponge, clear plastic wrap, small plastic knife, stamps, and stencils (B and C)

**Cleaning tools:** Warm soapy water

**Cleaning up spills:** If you accidentally go beyond the section to be textured when applying the gel medium, quickly clean up the excess with a clean or slightly damp cotton swab before the medium dries.

**Drying:** A thin coat takes several minutes to dry, while a thick coat will take several hours. As a general rule, if the coat is too thick, it may not ever dry completely and could remain white in the middle underneath the dried outer layer. In this case, pierce the undried sections with a needle to allow air to circulate through them.

**Fragility and care:** Do not scrub a textured surface once it's dry as doing so may damage it. Do not immerse the piece in water or hang it in an overly humid room, as the medium may become cloudy (although it will become clear again when it dries).

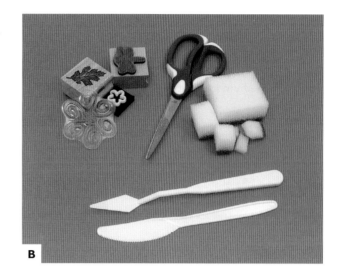

B

C

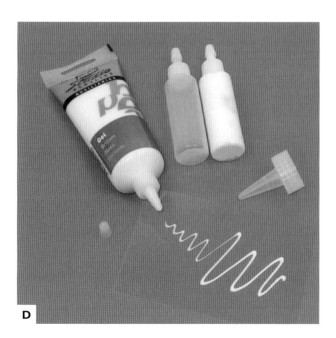

D

**Transferring the medium to an applicator bottle:** The textures in this chapter are made with many different tools. For some of them, if you are using gel medium from a jar instead of a tube with a pointed applicator tip, you will need to transfer the medium to an inexpensive plastic squeeze bottle (D).

**Colored textures:** All the textures can be painted any color once completely dry.

# How to make textures

## Embossed effect

**Tools: gel medium in a bottle**

**1.** Apply the gel medium unevenly through the whole section in small swirls going in all directions, leaving some small sections uncovered. Try to use the same kind of strokes throughout for a harmonious effect and avoid applying large blobs, which can take a long time to dry completely.

**2.** Once the section is filled, let it dry until the gel medium is completely transparent.

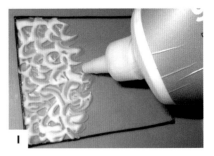

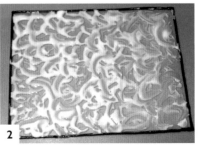

## Frosted effect

**Tools: squares of foam sponge cut into different sizes with scissors**

**1.** Dip a square of sponge in gel medium that's been squeezed into a scrap container and pat it to distribute the medium evenly.

**2.** Tap the sponge across the section to be textured to create a fine, delicate effect—you should see small bubbles everywhere.

**3.** Let dry.

**Tip:** You can use different kinds of sponges to vary the result. The finer the sponge, the finer the texture will be.

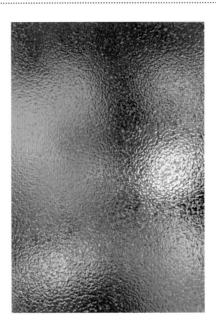

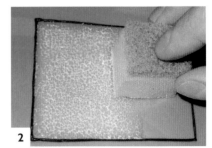

# Marbled effect

**Tools: palette knife and clear plastic wrap**

**1.** To create a marbled effect, use the palette knife to apply a thin coat of gel medium across the project's surface.

**2.** Next, place the plastic wrap over the gel and gently wrinkle it with your fingers. Remove the plastic wrap and check that the small wrinkle lines are visible throughout the section.

**3.** If the effect is not satisfactory, form a ball with the plastic wrap and use it to gently tap the gel medium to get the look you want.

**4.** Let dry.

**Tip:** Use a fresh piece of plastic wrap for each section, as it will quickly become covered with gel.

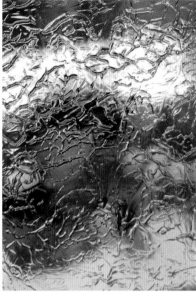

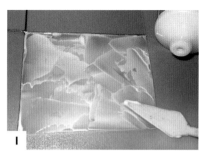

# Ripple effect

**Tools: palette knife**

**1.** Spread a thin coat of gel medium across the whole surface. Add "brush-strokes" with the palette knife evenly distributed across the section, taking care to not leave large peaks or blobs of the medium.

**2.** Let dry.

**Tip:** The palette knife must be smaller than the section you are covering with the gel.

## Wave effect

**Tools: small plastic knife with toothed edge and palette knife**

1. Cut off the end of the plastic knife blade with scissors—taking off the whole rounded part, if the knife is long enough.

2. Use the palette knife to spread a thin coat of gel medium over the whole section. Press part of the toothed edge of the knife into the gel medium and draw little waves about an inch long in the medium, going in all directions. If the teeth fill with medium, wipe them off with a paper towel. Continue in this way until the section is full of waves, all the way to the edges.

3. Let dry.

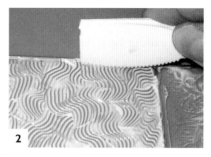

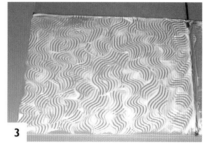

**Tip:** You can go back over previously made waves as long as the gel is still creamy and has not started to dry.

## Line effect

**Tools: small plastic knife with toothed edge and palette knife**

The line effect is often used for the outer edges of a stained glass painting because it is easier to handle the knife on these parts, but this effect can also be used on any other part of a project.

1. Use the palette knife to spread a thin coat of gel medium across the section.

2. Rest the toothed edge of the knife on the edge of the section and draw it straight across to create fine parallel lines; repeat until the section is completely filled. The lines should be straight and well defined. You will need to wipe the knife from time to time with a paper towel to remove the excess gel. If you are not satisfied with the pattern you get, spread the gel out again and start over.

3. Let dry.

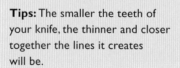

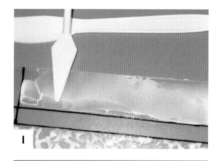

**Tips:** The smaller the teeth of your knife, the thinner and closer together the lines it creates will be.

If the rounded end of the knife makes it difficult to work, simply cut it off.

# Crisscross effect

**Tools: small plastic knife with toothed edge and palette knife**

**1.** Cut off the end of the plastic knife blade with scissors, taking off the whole rounded part, if the knife is long enough.

**2.** Use the palette knife to spread a thin coat of gel medium over the section.

**3.** Press the toothed edge of the knife into the gel medium and draw small sections of fine parallel lines about half an inch long in all directions, as shown. For a harmonious effect, the lines should cross at 90-degree angles and extend all the way to the edges. Wipe off excess gel medium from the knife with a paper towel as often as necessary.

**4.** Let dry.

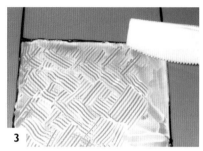

**Tip:** You can go over the lines again as long as the medium is still creamy.

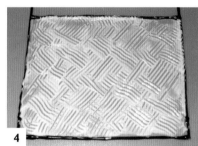

# Stucco effect

**Tools: palette knife**

**1.** Apply a medium-thick coat of gel medium over the whole section.

**2.** Pat the medium gently with the flat side of the palette knife to form small peaks. The thicker the gel, the larger the peaks will be.

**3.** Let dry.

**Tip:** Be careful not to let the coat of gel medium get too thick or it won't dry thoroughly.

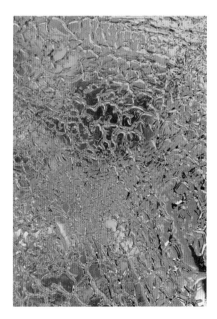

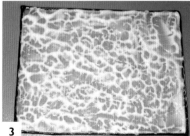

## *Stencil effect*

**Tools: stencil of your choice and palette knife**

Any kind of stencil can be used, metal or plastic, as long as it's smaller than the section being textured.

**1.** Start by creating a background texture across the surface—good background textures to use are ripple, frosted, or marbled. Let the texture dry completely.

**2.** Once the base texture is completely dry, place the stencil on the section and attach it securely in place, using tape if necessary. Make sure the stencil is held firmly against the surface or else the gel medium will leak out underneath it.

**3.** Use the palette knife to apply a thin coat of gel medium over the whole stencil pattern. This coat does not have to be particularly thick; the thickness of the stencil will be plenty. It is important here not to go over the same part too often or the medium will push out underneath the stencil.

**4.** Finally, gently lift the stencil with your hands and touch up the details of the design, using a toothpick or fine paintbrush, if necessary.

**5.** Let dry.

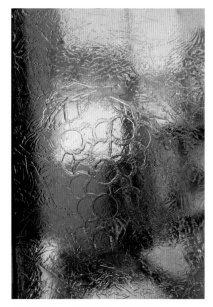

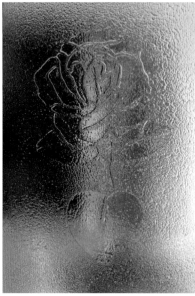

A stencil used on a frosted background

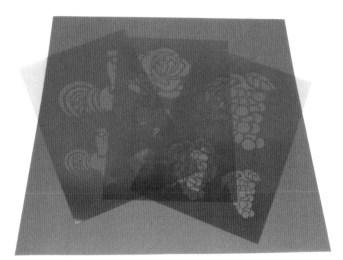

Examples of stencils

3

4

5

Stencil design on a marbled background

**Tips:** Clean the stencil with warm, soapy water as soon as you are finished using it.

If you need to, you can lightly spray the back of the stencil with a spray adhesive to help keep it in place.

You can use several stencils to make your design. You just have to wait for the first motif to dry before adding the next, if they touch.

If you find the stencil has moved too much and the design is ruined, wipe off the gel medium with a dry or damp rag (a white film will be left behind). Let the base dry completely and start again.

## *Stamped effect*

### Tools: Stamps of the designs of your choice

You can find stamps in craft and hobby stores. For this application, you can use stamps made of rubber, polymer, plastic, or foam, but they should not have too many small details. It is difficult at first to tell whether a design will look good when stamped; you have to try it out to see if you like the effect.

**1.** Start by creating a background texture across the whole surface. Good background textures to use with the stamped effect are ripple, frosted, or marbled. The other textures described here will not work as well because of the thickness of the gel medium they require.

**2.** As soon as the background texture is completed, stamp the motif where desired. Note that you can stamp several times with one stamp, but if you notice that the stamp is getting full of gel medium, wipe it off with a paper towel before continuing.

**3.** Once you've stamped all your desired motifs, let dry.

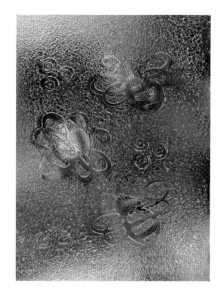

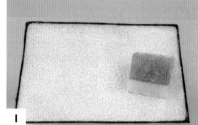

1

Frosted texture ready for stamping

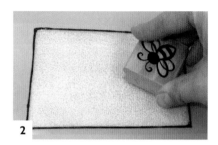

2

2

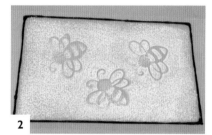

2

3

**Tips:** Clean the stamp in warm water using a toothbrush as soon as you are done using it.

If you are not satisfied with the effect you get, simply redo the base texture and stamp again (as long as the gel has not dried yet).

You can use several different stamps in the same section to create an original design.

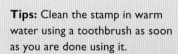

### Another example on a textured background

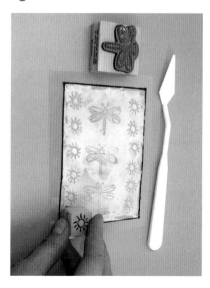

## Shatter effect

**Tools: palette knife**

1. Use the palette knife to spread a thin coat of gel medium all the way across the section then wipe off the palette knife with a paper towel.

2. Press the edge of the palette knife blade against the surface to make a mark in the medium. Create several imprints in this way right next to each other, in the shape of a fan.

Pivot the palette knife every time you make a mark. If the blade doesn't leave a mark in the surface, you either have too much or too little gel medium. Adjust the quantity accordingly.

3. Repeat the process nearby in another direction (it doesn't matter which), as shown, overlapping the fans. Continue to add overlapping fans all the way across the section to be textured. There should not be any empty spots.

4. Let dry.

**Tip:** You can go back over previously made marks as long as the gel medium is still creamy.

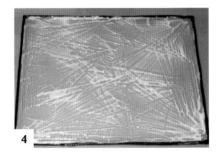

## Contour effect

**Tools: gel medium in a bottle with applicator tip**

This effect is added on top of another texture (the frosted effect, for example) to add dimension or clarity to it. To create it, simply outline a section or element of your project with the gel medium. You can vary the thickness of the line if you want a smaller or larger

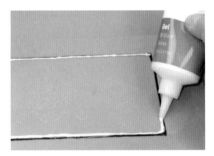

outline. Be careful, however, not to let the line get too thick because then it will not dry all the way through.

### So many possibilities!

It is possible to combine these textures on top of each other to create new effects. You must, however, wait for the first texture to dry completely before going on to the next one. Two examples of overlapping textures are shown here.

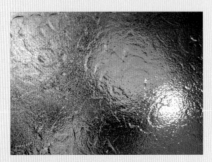

Frosted effect over embossed effect

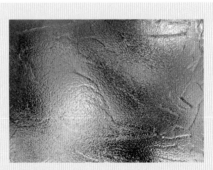

Frosted effect over ripple effect

# Upgrading a door

You can use texture effects to dramatically change the look of a door that has clear glass panes. However, I don't recommend you work directly on the panes—once the textures are created, they are very difficult to scrape off, and you might not even be able to preserve the door. A handy solution to this problem is to create the textures on sheets of acetate cut slightly larger than the panes of the door and insert them into each frame, replacing the glass (this also means you avoid having to take the door down).

Or you can also attach adhesive plastic film to the glass panes and paint on it. (In this case, you need to lay the door flat while you paint and make sure the paint doesn't touch the edges. Use a line of relief outliner that doesn't touch the frame if needed.)

These two solutions are fantastic, because they allow you to remove the motifs whenever you want to change the design, and the door stays intact.

In the example shown here, the idea was to simulate the look of old, uneven and frosted glass, so the ripple effect and frosted effect textures were created, one after the other, on rectangles of acetate. Next, I added different motifs with a stencil on half of the panes to give them another dimension. The acetate panes were then simply inserted into the frames of the door (4).

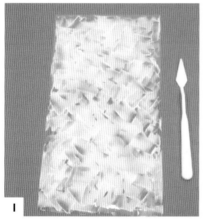

**1**

Ripple effect

**2**

Frosted effect

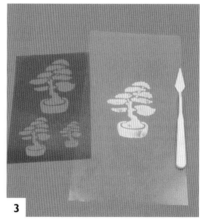

**3**

Stencil effect

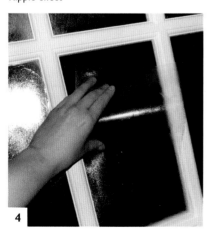

**4**

# Painting

- Introduction to glass paints
- Techniques for filling in the background
- Working with glitter medium
- Lightening a color
- How to create a gradient
- Creating special effects
- Drying, protection, and care

# Introduction to glass paints

You've prepared your surface, transferred the pattern, outlined the motif, and perhaps even added texture to your project. Now you are ready to paint. You will find in this chapter a summary of the main basic techniques used to color in specific sections of your project. Techniques for more advanced color mixing are described throughout the project sections in this book.

**Products used:** solvent-based glass paints
**Drying time:** 24 hours
**Cleaning paintbrushes:** odorless mineral spirits or solvent

## Basic techniques

Before starting to paint, it is important to use a few basic techniques if you want to get beautiful results:

**1.** No matter what surface you are working on, make sure it is perfectly level—a standard level tool will help with this. Glass paints are quite fluid, and the smallest slope can make the paint run to one side.

**2.** Stir the paint in the jars with a craft stick to make sure the color is uniformly mixed in. You should *not* shake the bottles, as this will leave lots of little bubbles in the paint.

**3.** Protect your work surface with a sheet of plastic. If you are working on a transparent surface such as glass, slide a piece of paper or light cardboard (white is best) underneath it so that the colors you're using show up well. If you are working on glass or plexiglass, do not place it directly on the table. Raise it slightly by laying it on top of plastic cups or similar small items. This will make it much easier to see if a section is completely colored in all the way to the edges.

**4.** All paintbrushes and other tools used with glass paints must be cleaned with a solvent. To clean them, pour a small amount of solvent into a scrap container. Each time you change colors, clean the brush in the solvent. Wipe it off on a paper towel, making sure there is neither paint nor solvent left on the paintbrush. Then go on to the next color.

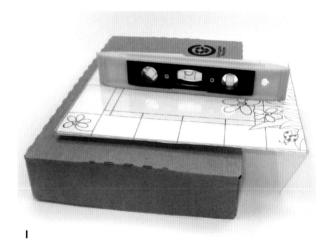

I

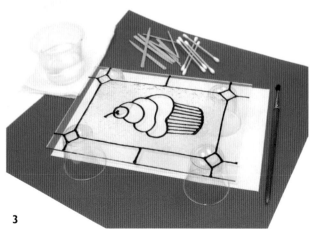

3

4

**5.** Quickly wipe up any paint that spills over the lines with a cotton swab before it dries. When the paint is completely dry, usually after 24 hours, it is impossible to remove.

**6.** Work in a well-ventilated area and leave only the jar you are currently using open. Keep the others closed.

**7.** Unless otherwise indicated, you can fill in specific sections of a stained glass painting in whatever order you like. The colors can always be changed. However, certain special effects can only be worked with the transparent colors of the product line. If you change these colors for opaque ones, you will not get the same effects, as these colors will not react in the same way.

**8.** Toothpicks are very useful for filling in small sections; don't forget to use them.

**9.** Some of the patterns in this book must be enlarged on a photocopier in order to use them in their proper size. (Of course, you can change the size or even adapt the patterns to use on a different piece than suggested.) Here is the formula for calculating the percentage to enlarge or reduce a pattern:

Divide the desired measurement by the measurement of the pattern and multiply this number by 100. For example, the pattern is 7 inches wide and you want to enlarge it to 11 inches wide; here is the calculation: $11 \div 7 \times 100 = 157$ percent.

The same is true for reduction. If you want to reduce a pattern that is 20 inches wide to 12 inches wide, reduce the pattern by $12 \div 20 \times 100$, or 60 percent.

**10.** When you are painting flat on a transparent surface such as glass, it is normal for the colors to appear darker when they're applied. When you put the window up to the light, the colors will be much lighter and brighter than on the table. A good way to make sure that the color is the one you want is to view the project against a light source from time to time as you work on it.

**11.** Any mixture containing white paint or pearlescent medium (also called iridescent medium) will appear dark when light shines through the glass—these paints block the light instead of letting it pass through. Keep this in mind when you plan out your design.

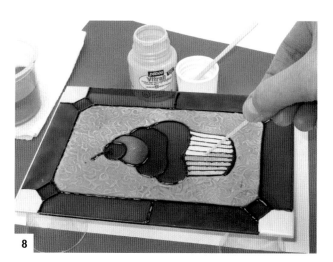

8

11

Super white paint against the light

# Techniques for painting untextured and textured sections

**The technique for painting a section that is not textured is not the same as the technique for painting a textured section. Here is how to proceed for each case.**

## Sections without texture

To create a uniformly colored section, it is necessary to use a lot of paint. Dip the entire head of the brush in the paint to fill the bristles. The size of the paintbrush depends on the size of the section you are going to fill but, as a general rule, a medium-sized brush (#6 or #8) works well. Once the brush is full of paint, place it gently on the section—without spreading the bristles out too much—to deposit the paint (1). Then lift up and reload the brush (2), and deposit the paint on the glass again. The goal is to gradually fill the section until the color evens itself out (3). Fill all the sections of one color in this way, then wash your brush and proceed to another color.

To fill small sections or spaces that are difficult to paint with a brush, use a toothpick or craft stick (4). If you go over the lines into another section while painting, simply wipe up the excess paint with a clean cotton swab before it dries.

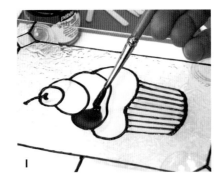

1

2

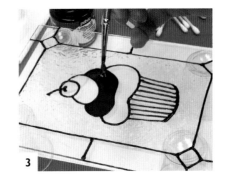

3

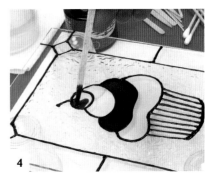

4

## Filling in a large section with color

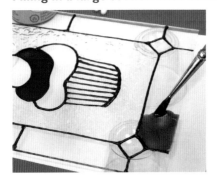

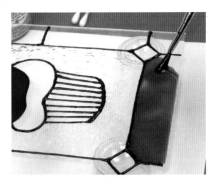

**Important:** I recommend that you avoid applying the paint in a thin coat; the color will not be even, and you will be able to see all the brushstrokes when the glass is held up to the light (E). Of course, this method can be interesting if you want an uneven effect, but this is not the desired look here.

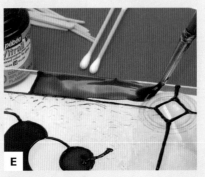

E

If you spread out the paint in a thin coat, you will see all the brushstrokes.

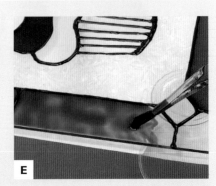

E

Not enough paint here—the color is uneven.

### Textured sections

To paint a textured section, simply paint the section as evenly as possible with the paintbrush. The coat of paint must be thick enough so that the brush-strokes are not visible but not so thick as to bury the texture entirely.

*Note that an embossed effect texture was previously applied to the central section of this project.*

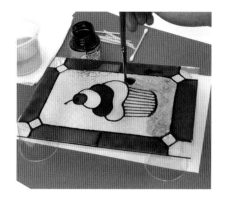
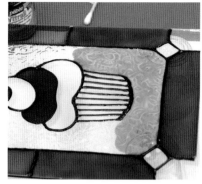

Close-up view

### Painting on canvas

If you are painting on canvas, you have more options for filling sections with color. In addition to using the basic technique for untextured surfaces, you can also use a paintbrush to spread a thin coat of paint over a section. This method will allow the texture of the canvas to show through the paint, which can give it interest and depth.

### What if you don't like the color?

**WET PAINT**

If you accidentally fill in a section with the wrong color, or change your mind after applying the paint, you can remove the paint with a cotton swab as long as it is still wet. (1, 2)

**DRY PAINT**

If the paint has dried, it's much more complicated. On surfaces with a white background, such as canvas or wood, you can cover the problem section with white opaque paint, let it dry, and paint over it with a new color.

On mirror, metal, acetate, or plexiglass, all you can do is add another layer of paint, using the new color; unfortunately, the new color will usually simply combine with the original one.

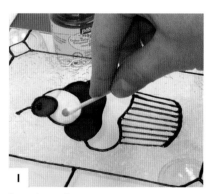

1

Example on glass

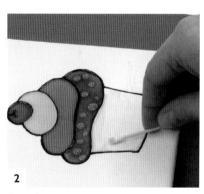

2

Example on canvas

On transparent glass, it all depends on the shape of the affected section. You can go around the edge of the section with a craft knife and then peel the paint, inserting the knife blade underneath the paint to lift it off. This process is very difficult, however, and sometimes impossible if the section is very small or full of details. (Note that this approach is not recommended for plexiglass, mirror, or acetate as it can damage them.)

Finally, as a last resort, you can immerse a piece of glass in water to try to detach the dried paint and save the piece. None of these solutions are a hundred percent effective—so take your time and choose your colors carefully before applying them.

# Working with glitter medium

**To add a touch of sparkle to your colors, use glitter medium—it contains small sparkles that create a shimmering effect.**

Glitter medium can be used alone just like regular glass paint or mixed with paint colors. It's important to mix it well before using, as the glitter often sinks to the bottom of the jar. Note that glass paint blended with glitter medium dries with a matte finish.

## How to make a blend

Pour the necessary amount of paint into a small container and add a few drops of glitter medium with a cotton swab (A). Mix gently with a craft stick, making sure the amount of glitter is what you want. If not, add a little more. Be careful—the more glitter medium you add to the color, the lighter the color will become. Fill in the chosen section with the blend (B, C).

**A**

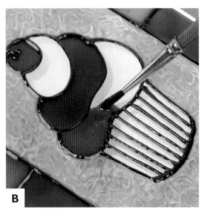

**B**

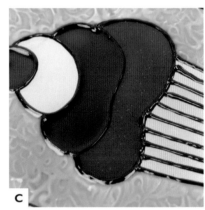

**C**

**Note:** Remember that the paint blend will not sparkle when the project is held against the light. The look will be more like that of sand in the paint (F). On the other hand, the glitter will be very apparent against an opaque background such as mirror or canvas.

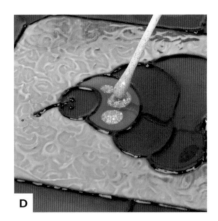

**D**

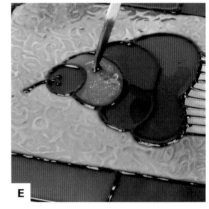

**E**

**F**

## Working directly on a surface

You can also mix the blend right on your project surface if you don't need much paint. Just fill in the chosen section with the glass paint and then use a cotton swab to add a few drops of glitter medium to it (D). Mix everything together very carefully.

# Lightening a color

**You can lighten a color that is too dark to create different shades. To do this, you need to add lightening medium to it. Here's how:**

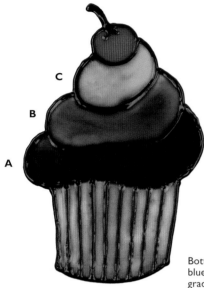

Pour the desired amount of paint into a small container. Use a cotton swab to add lightening medium and mix gently with a craft stick—do not shake the mixture. The amount of medium to add depends on the shade you want. The more medium you add, the lighter and more transparent the color will be. I strongly suggest, therefore, that you do some preliminary tests to make sure the result is what you want.

You can use lightening medium alone, just like regular glass paint. You can also use it to varnish a piece and give shine to a matte color.

Bottom layer of frosting (A): original color (turquoise blue). Top and center layers (C, B): same color but gradually lightened with lightening medium.

# How to create a gradient

**There are many ways to create a gradient effect. Here are some possibilities.**

## Gradient with several colors

Paint the chosen section, placing the desired colors side by side. The colors must touch each other, and you must put enough paint down so they don't dry before you've finished working all of them (A). It's important to work quickly. Once the colors have all been applied, blend each transition gently with a small toothpick or paintbrush, making swirls in all directions. Be careful to leave some of each color untouched (B). Let dry (C).

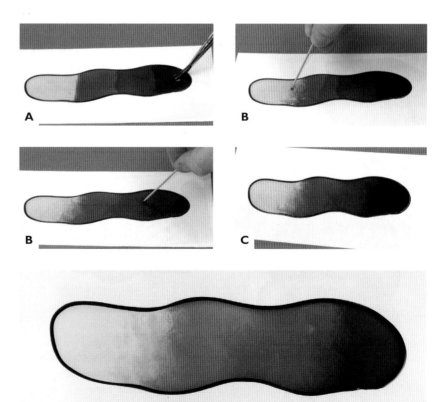

Close-up view of blending

Against the light

## Making a shaded leaf

To create a leaf that shades from dark at the base to lighter at the tip, there are several methods you could use.

You can add lightening medium directly to the color to lighten certain parts.

You can also work with two different foundation colors in the same family (apple green and chartreuse, for example—two different kinds of green). One should be dark and the other lighter. Simply fill in the appropriate sections with the two colors, making sure they touch in the middle (A, B). Use a paintbrush or toothpick to gently swirl the colors where they meet. Wipe off the brush on a paper towel then lighten the tip of the leaf by touching the brush to it so that the bristles pull up some of the paint (C). Let dry.

How it looks against the light

**A**

Apple green

**B**

Chartreuse

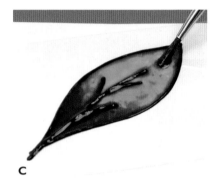

**C**

## Glittery gradient

Here's another method for making a background of multiple colors, but this time with a touch of sparkle. Start by painting the sections with the desired colors. Work gradually, adding them one by one (A, B). Use a swab to add a few drops of glitter medium to the paint surface (C). Finally, swirl the colors and medium together with the tip of a paintbrush until you are happy with the result (D). Let dry.

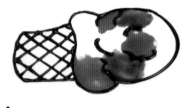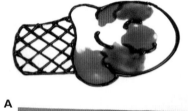

**A**

**B**

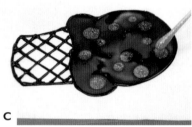

**C**

**D**

How it looks against the light

### The secret of a good gradient

It doesn't matter which technique you use to create a gradient; what is important is that you apply enough paint in the background that it doesn't dry before you're finished creating the effect.

# *Creating colorful mixes and effects*

**You can create lots of colorful effects with the various transparent colors and mediums available to you. These effects are fun to make, since there are a multitude of possibilities. Because colors and mediums do not all react the same way, you're likely to create some surprises.**

To create a fun mix, first paint a section with the color of your choice (1). For example, all the sections of this design were filled in with different colors. Go wherever your imagination takes you!

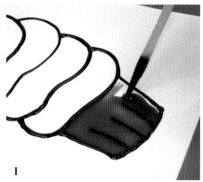

1

Paint all the sections with the colors of your choice.

**Some examples:**

A - A few drops of lightening medium on the base color

B - Drops of glitter medium

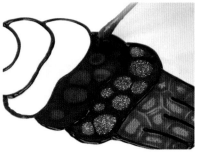

C - Drops of another color (in this case, lemon)

D - Drops of white (not super white)

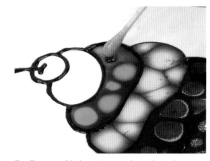

E - Drops of lightening medium (another result)

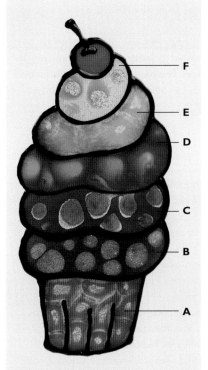

**A:** Yellow base
**B:** Cobalt blue base
**C:** Parma base
**D:** Crimson base
**E:** Apple green base
**F:** Lemon base

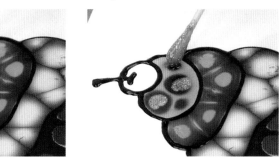

F - Drops of another color (sky blue) with drops of glitter medium on top

# Drying, protection, and care

## Drying

Glass paint generally takes 24 hours to dry completely, but it can take even longer if the paint has been applied very thickly.

To prevent dust from settling on your project while the paint dries (it will stay sticky for several hours), cover it with a piece of stiff, clean cardboard. Do *not* put the project in an airtight container while it dries, however.

You can uncover the project when the paint is smooth to the touch, no longer tacky.

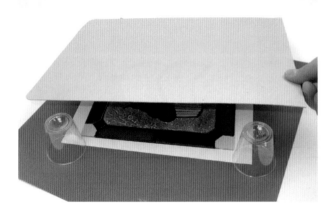

## Protection

It is not necessary to varnish your stained glass painting, because the paint itself is fairly resistant. I never varnish my decorative stained glass pieces, and they have survived the years very well. But if the project will see frequent use, or if it will be displayed in a place where it could be damaged, it is a good idea to apply a coat of extra protection.

There are several products you can use to varnish a project. The important thing to remember is that if your glass paint is solvent based, you must use a solvent-based varnish over it. For example, you can apply a coat of lightening medium over the project (keeping in mind that lightening medium yellows a bit with age and can change the colors of your project, especially if you have white sections).

You can also apply a coat of epoxy varnish, which is lighter than lightening medium. There are also other oil-based varnishes on the market with UV protection; I recommend that you first test their compatibility with glass paint before using them.

## Care

Although stained glass paintings look like real works of stained glass, they are not as durable. They are not designed to be used outdoors.

Do not immerse the project in water and avoid displaying it in extremely humid places. The paint can crack and even peel over time. A damp cloth can be used to clean your project of any dust.

I do not recommend painting directly on an exterior window, even if the paint is applied on the inside. Frost, thawing, condensation, cold, and so on can damage the paint. The best way to decorate an exterior window is to hang the stained glass painting inside, in front of the window, leaving a bit of space between the window and the project. The same goes for a door to a shower.

You can, of course, hang a stained glass painting outside, but it will likely not remain in good condition for very long. How long depends on exposure—whether it's in the open or a sheltered area (for example, under a roof overhang where it will not get rained on). A plaque hung near a wall, sheltered from the sun and wind, will not be damaged as quickly as a plaque hung right in the middle of a garden. It's up to you to decide whether your project will need to be coated with a UV protector or waterproofed front and back.

# 25 Projects to Make!

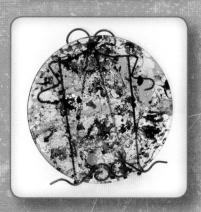

This chapter features 25 stained glass painting projects involving all kinds of different surfaces. Through these projects, you will learn how to correctly use the techniques described in the previous chapters while also discovering new, more advanced techniques.

*Certain basic instructions, such as preparing surfaces, outlining the design, textures, and filling in sections, have been simplified here in the interests of streamlining the text. For each of these steps, please refer to the preceding chapters if you need more information.*

# 25 Projects to make!

**1**
Sparkling rose
52

**2**
Art deco tulips
55

**3**
Favorite frame
58

**7**
Stained glass with sticker
68

**8**
Multicolored butterfly
71

**9**
Lighted glass block
76

**13**
Dare to go transparent
90

**14**
Tea Time
92

**15**
Elongated format
95

**20**
Kitten mirror
108

**21**
Peace tortoise
110

**22**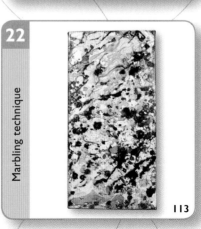
Marbling technique
113

# 25 Projects to make!

**4** A flower for you

61

**5** Cupcake (relief outliner version)

64

**6** Cupcake (lead strip version)

66

**10** Red tulips

79

**11** Colored glass tiles

85

**12** Art deco panel

88

**16** Decorative plaques

**17** **18**
98, 100, 103

**19** Elegant mirror

105

**23** Stained-glass greeting cards

116

**24** Color me bold!
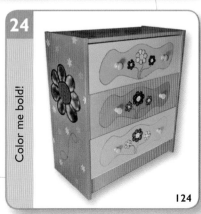
124

**25** Cupcake (canvas version)

128

## Materials

**Pattern:** Page 140
**Surface:** Glass
**Measurements:** 9 x 12 in.

**Colors used:**
Sky blue, chartreuse, lemon,
crimson, orange

**Other products:**
Relief outliner: black
Glitter medium
Gloss gel medium

**Textures:**
Embossed effect, frosted
effect

**Other materials:**
Small container

## Preparing the piece

**1.** Clean the pane of glass with rubbing alcohol and a paper towel.

## Positioning the pattern

**2.** Place the pattern under the glass and attach it firmly at the top and bottom with tape.

## Outlining the design

**3.** Cover all the lines of the design—except the outer edge—with a relief outline.

## Adding texture

**4.** Create the embossed and frosted textures in the shaded sections as shown in the diagrams. Let dry until the medium is completely clear. Then go on to the painting step.

### Tip

See chapter 5 for directions on creating the textures used in all these projects.

Embossed effect diagram

Frosted effect diagram

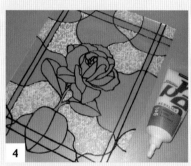

Embossed effect

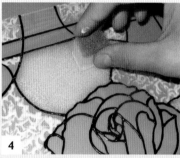

Frosted effect

## Painting

This project is divided into three parts: the greenery, the rose, and the background sections. Do them one by one. Once the parts are completed, let dry for 24 hours, protected from dust.

### *Leaves and stem*

*Chartreuse and glitter medium*

The three leaves are painted one at a time.

**5.** With a paintbrush, paint all the sections of one leaf with chartreuse. As soon as the sections are filled, add a few drops of glitter medium onto the wet paint.

**6.** Mix the paint and glitter medium gently with the tip of the paintbrush,

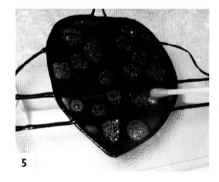

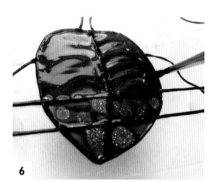

going in the direction of the leaf. Add more medium as needed. Let dry.

**7.** Repeat for the other two leaves.

The stem is simply filled in with chartreuse. Use a toothpick.

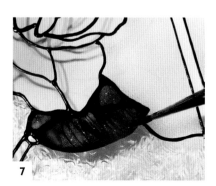

## Rose

*Crimson (C), orange (O), glitter medium*

Paint the petals one at a time, as you'll want to create a multicolored foundation in each one. See the diagram below for the colors for each petal (the dotted lines indicate where the colors meet). Simply fill in the small sections with a single color using a toothpick. Here is how to proceed:

**8.** First paint one petal with the two foundation colors—crimson (C) and orange (O)—making sure the two colors meet.

**9.** Next, dip a clean cotton swab in the glitter medium and add a few drops to the petal—especially at the tip—to lighten it slightly.

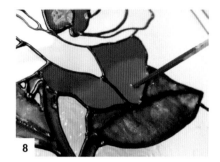

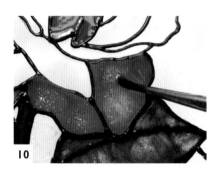

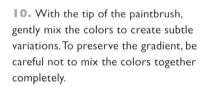

**10.** With the tip of the paintbrush, gently mix the colors to create subtle variations. To preserve the gradient, be careful not to mix the colors together completely.

**11.** Repeat for all the petals, following the diagram. You can paint several petals at once as long as you work quickly.

### Color key

(see the pattern)

**J** = Blend of lemon and a touch of orange
**O** = Orange
**V** = Chartreuse
**B** = Sky blue
**C** = Crimson

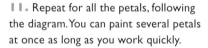

## The background

**12.** Paint all the background sections with the colors indicated on the pattern (see the key at left). Use toothpicks for small sections and a paintbrush for the larger ones. And use a paintbrush for all the textured sections, as you need to spread a thin coat of paint over the texture.

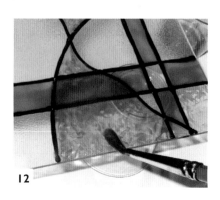

## Materials

**Pattern:** Page 141
**Surface:** Glass
**Measurements:** 8 x 12 in.

**Colors used:**
Cobalt blue, lemon, salmon, apple green

**Other products:**
Adhesive lead strip
Gloss gel medium

**Textures:**
Embossed effect, frosted effect

## Preparing the piece

1. Clean the glass with rubbing alcohol and a paper towel.

## Positioning the pattern

2. Place the pattern under the pane of glass and attach it securely at the top and bottom with tape.

## Outlining the design

3. Apply adhesive lead strips over all the lines of the design, except the outside edge. For best results, outline the elements in this order:

1—Leaves (2)
2—Stems (3), over the bases of the leaves
3—Tulips (3), start at the tops and end with the rounded bases
4—Small short lines that separate the border sections (6)
5—Long horizontal lines (2)
6—Long vertical lines (2)

panel (the light gray section in the diagram) to form a frame about half an inch wide around the design.

5. As soon as you have finished with the embossed frame, create a frosted effect on the rest of the background. Make sure the line where the two textures meet is straight and uniform as it will be fairly prominent once the project is dry.

6. Once the two textures are finished, wipe off the medium right along the edges of the lines of the tulips and leaves with clean cotton swabs. Do your best to get all the medium off, as this border should be clear and will be prominent too once the medium is dry. If the medium has begun to dry and is hard to remove, wet a swab with a little water and rub. The gel will likely come off more easily.

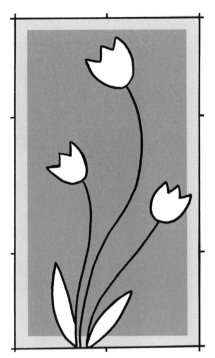

Embossed effect: light gray
Frosted effect: dark gray

3

## Adding texture

Add texture to the design as indicated in the following instructions. Let dry completely, until the gel is completely clear.

## *Central section*

The central section contains two textures and a clear border surrounding the tulip and leaves. These three steps should be done one after the other. Work quickly so the gel medium doesn't dry before you finish.

4. Start by creating the embossed effect all the way around the central

4

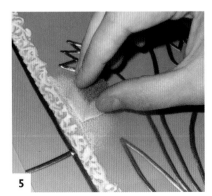

5

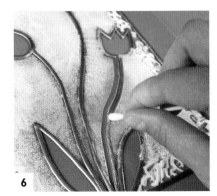

6

## Other sections

*Frosted effect (sections in gray, near right)*

**7.** Create the frosted texture in the four corner squares first.

**8.** The two middle sections are slightly different: add the frosted texture through the whole section, then quickly wipe off the medium right along the section's inside edges to create a clearly defined border.

Don't hesitate to use as many cotton swabs as you need to remove the medium. This border, the width of a cotton swab head, must be clean and well defined. If the medium becomes hard to remove, moisten the cotton swab with a little water.

Frosted effect

Embossed effect

*Embossed effect (sections in gray, far right)*

**9.** Create the embossed effect in all the sections indicated in the diagram. Let the project dry completely before moving on to the next step.

### Painting

**10.** Paint all the sections with the colors indicated on the pattern (see the key, below right). Toothpicks work best for filling in the small sections, such as the tulips and leaves.

**11.** To paint over a textured section, use a paintbrush to spread a thin coat of paint over the whole section.

8

10

Filling in a section with a toothpick

### A trick

Adhesive lead strip will become oxidized over time. If you don't want this to happen on your project, cover all the lead strip with lightening medium or clear varnish as soon as you finish the project. The silvery look of the strip will be lost as soon as you apply the medium, but the lead will remain a uniform dark color.

11

Painting on textured glass

### Color key

(see the pattern)

**S** = Salmon
**C** = Lemon
**B** = Cobalt blue
**V** = Apple green

*Favorite frame*

Back view

## Materials

**Pattern:** Page 142
**Surface:** Plexiglass photo frame
**Measurements:** 8 x 10 in.

**Colors used:**
Turquoise blue, black, blue jeans, ocean blue, sun yellow, red, light green

**Other products:**
Lightening medium
Relief outliner: black

**Other materials:**
Toothpicks
A favorite photo

## Preparing the piece

**1.** Clean the surface with a paper towel to remove any dust.

## Positioning the pattern

**2.** Place the pattern under the frame and attach it securely at the top and bottom with tape. Prop the frame up on something so it sits level.

## Outlining the design

**3.** Cover all the lines of the design, including the outer edge, with relief outliner.

## Painting

**4.** Paint all the sections with the colors indicated in the pattern and key. Use toothpicks to fill in the small sections. The greenery and outer frame sections have special instructions, given below.

**Color key**

(see the pattern)

**O** = Ocean blue
**B** = Blue jeans
**R** = Red
**N** = Black

Note: The centers of the flowers are not painted.

4

## *Greenery section*

*Light green (V), Sun yellow and light green (VJ)*

**5.** With a large toothpick, fill in all the sections of the greenery marked V or VJ on the pattern with the light green paint.

**6.** Next, quickly add a drop of sun yellow paint to all the sections marked VJ and swirl the colors with a toothpick. You want to create a different green in these sections. Let dry.

6

## Outer frame

*Turquoise blue and lightening medium (E)*

It is important that the frame be level while you create this effect. All the sections of the outer frame (E) are filled in the same way. You should still do them one at a time, however, as the paint cannot be allowed to dry until the effect is completed.

**7.** With a paintbrush, apply a generous coat of turquoise blue paint to fill the whole section.

**8.** Once the section is filled, use a cotton swab to add small drops of lightening medium close together across the section. Be careful not to drown the section in lightening medium or the effect will be lost; you just want some small circles of lighter color within the darker background.

**9.** Repeat this process in the other sections, then let dry for 24 hours in a well-ventilated place.

**To get the full impact of the special effect in this frame, make sure to place the photo behind only the central part.**

7

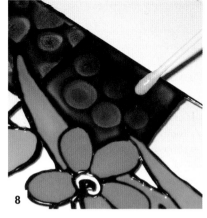

8

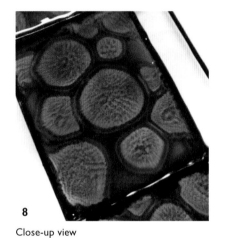

8

Close-up view

### Variation

Change the colors, change the style!

You can adapt this project for any plexiglass frame on the market. It can be worked on a glass frame, too.

9

## Materials

**Pattern:** Page 143
**Surface:** Glass
**Measurements:** 8 x 10 in.

**Colors used:**
Ocean blue, clementine, wheat yellow, red, light green

**Other products:**
Relief outliner: black
Gloss gel medium

**Textures:**
Embossed effect, frosted effect

**Other materials:**
Large toothpicks

## Preparing the piece

**1.** Clean the glass with rubbing alcohol and a paper towel.

## Positioning the pattern

**2.** Place the pattern under the glass and attach it securely at the top and bottom with tape.

## Outlining the design

**3.** Cover all the lines of the design, except the dashed lines on the pattern, with the relief outliner.

## Painting

**4.** Paint all the sections except the petals and leaves with the colors indicated in the pattern and color key. It's best to use toothpicks to fill in these sections. Note that the petals and leaves are worked differently (see below).

Once you've painted the sections, let dry completely before moving on to the next step.

## *Flower petals*

*Red (R), clementine (C)*

All the petals contain two colors and are painted in the same way (see the pattern).

**5.** With a large toothpick, fill in the section of the flower petal closest to the center with red, stopping at the dashed line.

**6.** Next, fill in the rest of the section with clementine.

**7.** Gently blend the transition between the two colors to form a gradient. Let dry.

**8.** Repeat this process for the other petals. You can fill in several petals at once, as long as you work quickly.

**4**

Filling in the light green (V) sections.

**4**

Filling in the clementine (C) sections.

### Color key

(see the pattern)

**B** = Ocean blue
**C** = Clementine
**J** = Wheat yellow
**V** = Light green

### Painting tip

Don't hesitate to apply the paint right up to the edge of the glass. Even though it might seem odd to do so, the paint will stay in place and will not run over the edge.

**5**

**6**

**7**

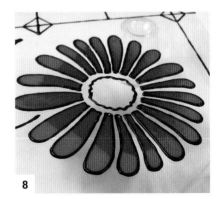

**8**

## Two leaves

*Light green (V), ocean blue (B)*

The leaves are worked just like the petals but with two different colors (see the pattern for placement).

**9.** With a large toothpick, fill in the base of the leaf with ocean blue (B), without going past the dashed line.

**10.** Next, fill in the rest of the leaf with light green (V).

**11.** Blend the transition between the two colors with the tip of the toothpick to create a smooth gradient. Let dry. Repeat the process on the second leaf, referring to the pattern for placement of the two colors.

### Finishing touches and painting the flower center

Add textures to the center and background as described below (see the pattern for placement). Let dry completely, until the gel medium becomes clear.

## Flower center

*Embossed effect (X)*

**12.** Create the embossed effect in the center of the flower. When the gel medium is completely dry and clear, paint the section ocean blue.

## Central background

*Frosted effect (Y)*

**13.** To create the frosted effect in between the petals, you'll need to use a tiny bit of sponge, as these sections are very small.

**14.** Apply the gel medium quickly to the rest of the background; as soon as you finish, wipe away the medium right along the inside border with a cotton swab to keep this section clear.

Use as many cotton swabs as you need to remove the gel. The clear border, the width of a cotton swab head, should be

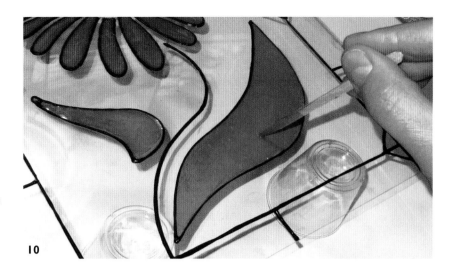

10

### Painting tip

When working with opaque colors, it's important to hold the project up against a light source from time to time as you paint to check that the effect is what you want. Viewed flat from the top, the project won't look the same as when it's backlit. Looking at it from below against a light, you can see if the effect you've achieved is what you are going for.

12

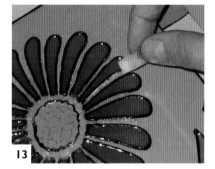

13

14

very well defined. If the gel becomes difficult to remove, moisten the cotton swab with a bit of water and rub.

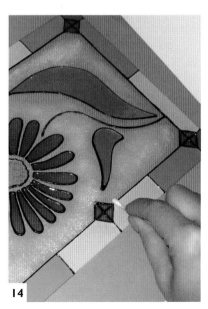

14

Cupcake (relief outliner version)

## Materials

**Pattern:** Page 144
**Surface:** Glass (from a small photo frame)
**Measurements:** 5 x 7 in.

**Colors used:**
Sky blue, cobalt blue, crimson, yellow, pink, wheat yellow, apple green

**Other products:**
Relief outliner: black
Glitter medium
Gloss gel medium

**Texture:**
Embossed effect

**Other materials:**
Small containers

## Preparing the piece

**1.** Clean the glass with rubbing alcohol and a paper towel.

## Positioning the pattern

**2.** Place the pattern under the glass and attach it securely at the top and bottom with tape.

## Outlining the design

**3.** Cover all the lines of the design, except the outer edge, with the relief outliner.

## Adding texture

**4.** Create an embossed effect in the central background section (marked with a V on the pattern) and let dry completely, until the medium is clear. Then go on to the next step.

## Painting

**5.** Paint all the sections with the colors indicated (see the pattern and key). Use toothpicks to fill in the small sections and a paintbrush for the larger ones.

For the textured section, use the paintbrush to spread a thin coat of paint over the texture.

Let the project dry completely, protected from dust.

### Color key

(see the pattern)

**B** = Cobalt blue
**J** = Wheat yellow
**R** = Pink
**C** = Crimson
**V** = Apple green
**Y** = Yellow
**M1** = Blend 1: half sky blue and half glitter medium
**M2** = Blend 2: half crimson and half glitter medium

4

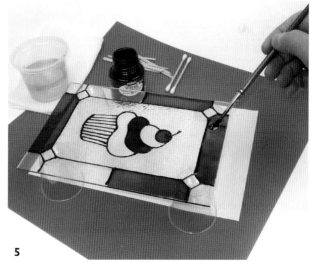

5

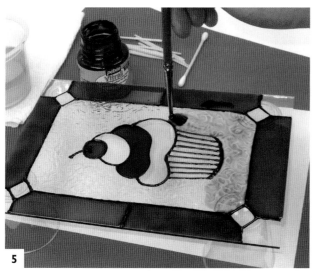

5

5

## 6

*Cupcake (lead strip version)*

## Materials

**Pattern:** Page 145
**Surface:** Glass (from a small photo frame)
**Measurements:** 8 x 8 in.

**Colors used:**
Sky blue, crimson, lemon, pink, apple green, orange

**Other products:**
Adhesive lead strips
Glitter medium
Gloss gel medium

**Texture:**
Embossed effect

**Other materials:**
Small container

## Preparing the piece

1. Clean the glass with rubbing alcohol and a paper towel.

## Positioning the pattern

2. Place the pattern under the glass and attach it securely at the top and bottom with tape.

## Outlining the design

3. Use adhesive lead strips to outline all the lines of the design—except for the outer edge.

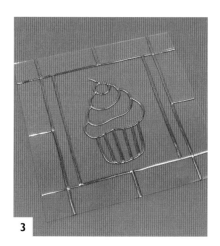

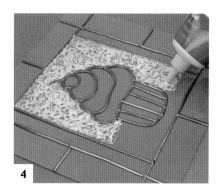

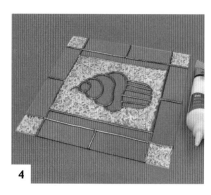

## Painting

5. Paint all the sections with the colors indicated (see the pattern and key). Use toothpicks to fill in the small sections, and a paintbrush for the larger sections.

Note that the textured sections are not painted in this project in order to highlight the textures themselves. Of course, if you want to add a color on top of the texture, you can do so.

Once the project is painted, let it dry for 24 hours, protected from dust.

### Color key

(see the pattern)

**C** = Crimson
**M1** = Blend 1: half sky blue and half glitter medium
**M2** = Crimson with drops of glitter medium; let dry as is
**V** = Apple green
**J** = Lemon
**R** = Pink
**O** = Orange

## Adding texture

4. Create an embossed effect in the shaded sections on the diagram. Let dry completely, until the medium becomes clear. Then go on to the next step.

Embossed effect diagram

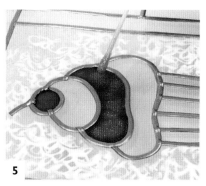

Adding glitter medium to the crimson

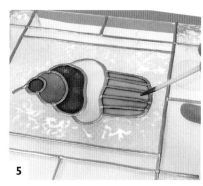

Painting the cup

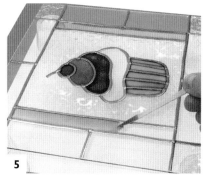

Filling in with the lemon

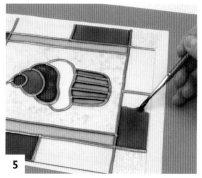

Completing the background

# Stained glass with sticker

## Materials

**Pattern:** Page 146
**Surface:** Glass
**Measurements:** 11 x 14 in.

**Colors used:**
Crimson, yellow, orange, apple green

**Other products:**
Relief outliner: gold
Glitter medium
Gloss gel medium

**Textures:**
Embossed effect, frosted effect

**Other materials:**
Gold peel-off sticker (a selection from the Starform Outline line is used here)
Craft knife

This project makes use of a combination of textures, paint, and stickers.

The idea is to create your own design, using a sticker of your choice in the central section.

You can also modify the colors of this project to match your decor.

## Preparing the piece

**1.** Clean the glass with rubbing alcohol and a paper towel.

## Positioning the pattern

**2.** Place the pattern under the glass and attach it securely at the top and bottom with tape.

## Outlining the design

**3.** Cover all the lines of the design—except the outer edge—with the relief outliner.

## Applying the stickers

**4.** Once the lines of relief outliner are completely dry, begin the central design. Place your selected outline sticker in the central section, making sure to press firmly on every part of the design.

**Be careful:** This step is very delicate and requires great care. Once the stickers are attached to the glass, it is very difficult to reposition them without tearing them. Once you've finished applying them, go on to the next step.

## Adding texture

**5.** Next, create an embossed effect texture in all the sections indicated by shaded sections on the diagram. Let dry until the gel medium is completely clear. Go on to the painting step.

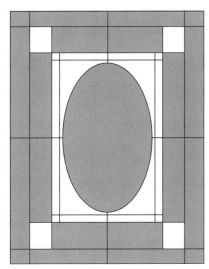

Embossed effect diagram

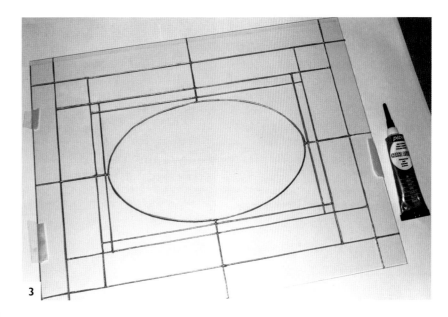

3

4

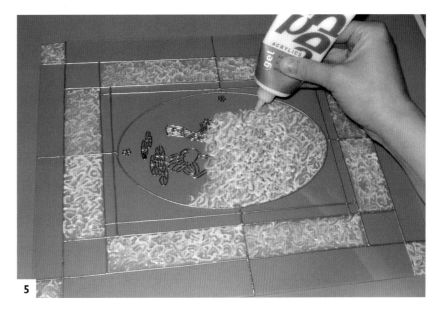

5

## Painting

**6.** Paint all the sections with the colors indicated (see the pattern and key). Use toothpicks for the small sections and a paintbrush for the larger ones. For the textured sections, use a paintbrush to spread a thin coat of paint over the texture. Let dry completely for 24 hours before moving on to the finishing step.

6

### Color key

(see the pattern)

**V** = Apple green
**O** = Orange
**C** = Crimson
**J** = Yellow

**Be careful not to paint over the relief outliner when painting the sections. If you do get some paint on the outlines, wipe it off before it dries.**

### Tip

It is important to always add a texture over stickers so they don't peel off with time.

Stickers are sold in many colors—you can use a color of relief outliner to match.

### Finishing touches with gloss gel medium
*Frosted effect*

**7.** Once the paint is dry, create a frosted effect in the central section (on top of the embossed effect).

**8.** As soon as the texture is created, quickly wipe off the medium along the inside of the border line with a clean cotton swab to create a clearly defined outline.

**9.** Let everything dry completely.

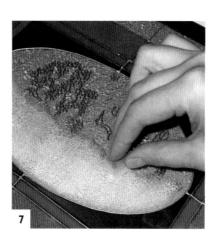

7

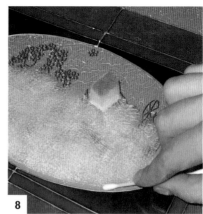

8

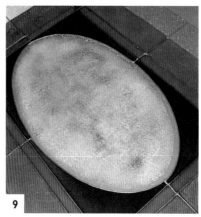

9

## Materials

**Pattern:** Page 147
**Surface:** Glass
**Measurements:** 14 x 11 in.

**Colors used:**
Sky blue, chartreuse, lemon, crimson, gold, orange

**Other products:**
Relief outliner: black
Glitter medium
Gloss gel medium

**Texture:**
Frosted effect

## Preparing the piece

1. Clean the glass with rubbing alcohol and a paper towel.

## Positioning the pattern

2. Place the pattern under the glass and attach it securely at the top and bottom with tape.

## Outlining the design

3. Cover all the lines of the design—except the dashed lines—with relief outliner.

## Adding texture

*Using gloss gel medium and squares of sponge about ¾ inch wide*

The background texture is created in two steps: It's a frosted effect finished off with a textured border. These two steps are worked one after the other, and it's important to work quickly so

that the medium doesn't dry before you're finished. Here is how to proceed:

4. Use a sponge dipped in the gel medium to create a frosted effect over the entire background section (not the butterfly). You need to work quickly because the medium cannot be allowed to dry before you get to the next step.

5. As soon as the texture is finished and while it is still wet, place the sponge flat about ¾ inch from the edge of the glass (indicated by dashed lines on the pattern) and slide it gently toward the edge to create fine lines in the medium. Work carefully, as this border should be very neat.

Repeat this process all the way around the glass to create a "striped" frame around the frosted section.

6. Let dry until the medium becomes clear. Then go on to the next step.

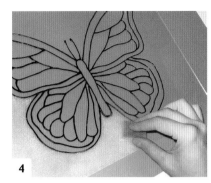

4

Frosted effect

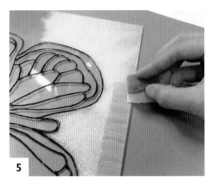

5

Finishing border

## Painting

The butterfly is divided into six sections: A, B, C, D, E, and F (see the pattern for color placement). I recommend you use large toothpicks to fill all these sections. The steps for a single section are worked one after the other—don't let the paint dry in between steps. Once all the sections of the butterfly are filled in, let the project dry for 24 hours, protected from dust.

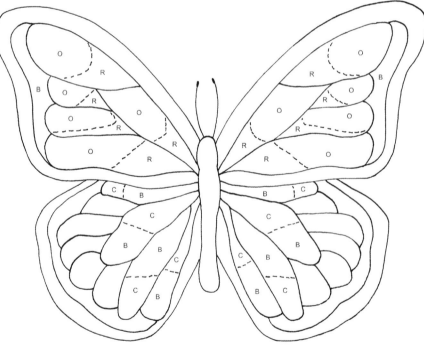

**Tip**

For great-looking effects, the paint must be fresh and still wet.

## A sections

*Sky blue (B), crimson (C), lemon, and glitter medium*

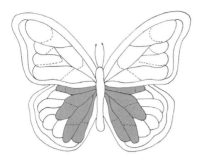

Start on the right side of the butterfly (the left side is an identical mirror image).

**7.** Paint a section with the sky blue and crimson. The dashed lines indicate the border between the two colors (note that the position of these colors is switched in each section).

**8.** Drop a few drops of lemon to the whole section.

**9.** Add a few drops of glitter medium to the whole section.

**10.** Mix the transition between the colors just a bit to create a swirly gradient effect.

**11.** Finish by adding a few more drops of glitter medium along the length of the section. Let the section dry as is.

**12.** Repeat these steps in all the other sections on the right side, switching the position of the foundation colors (sky blue and crimson) in every other section.

Repeat the process on the left side of the butterfly.

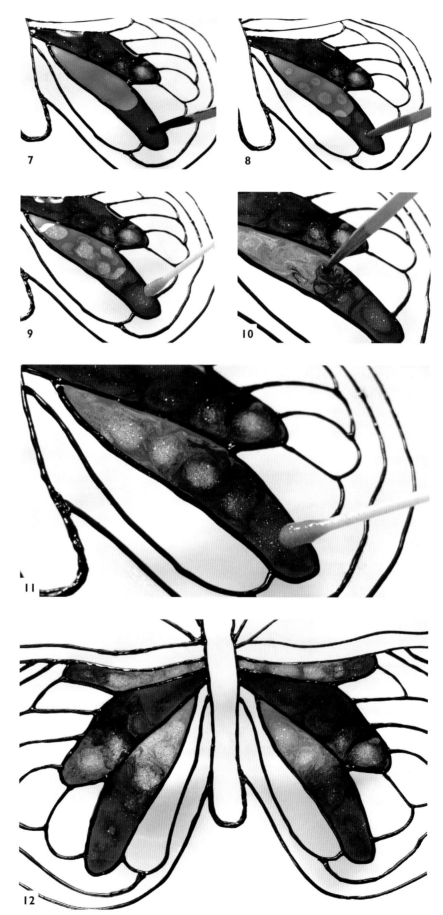

## B sections

*Gold (R), orange (O), crimson, and glitter medium*

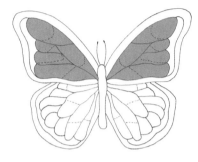

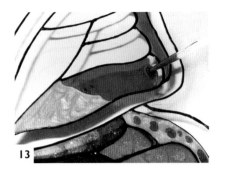

**13**

**14**

Start with the right side (the left side is an identical mirror image).

**13.** Fill in a section with gold and orange. The dashed lines on the pattern indicate where the two colors meet.

**14.** Blend the transition between the two colors to form a gradient.

**15.** Add a few drops of gold along the length of the section. The drops should get bigger as you move from the narrow end of the section to the wider end.

**16.** In each of these circles, add a drop of orange, then a drop of glitter medium.

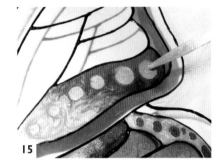

**15**

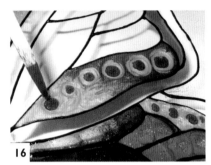

**16**

**17.** Finish by adding a tiny drop of crimson to each circle. Let dry as is.

Next, repeat these steps on the other sections within the B sections, then on the other side of the butterfly.

**18.** Note that you can fill in multiple sections at once if you work quickly.

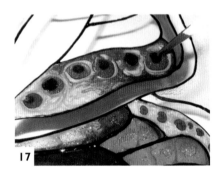

**17**

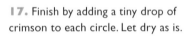

## C sections

*Lemon, sky blue, and glitter medium*

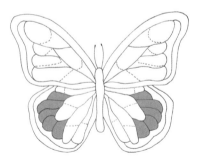

Start by painting the right side of the butterfly (the left side is an identical mirror image).

**19.** First, fill in the lemon sections.

**20.** Next, drop three drops of sky blue in each section, starting at the right.

**21.** Finally, add a drop of glitter medium on top of each blue circle, again starting at the right. Let dry as is.

Repeat these steps on the other side of the butterfly.

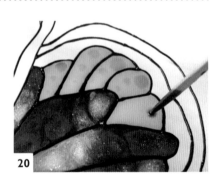

**20**

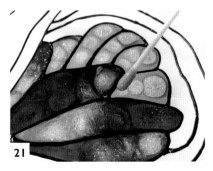

**21**

## D sections

*Gold and orange*

You can work these two sides at the same time.

**22.** First, fill in each section with gold paint.

**23.** Add drops of orange paint of varying sizes along the whole section. Let dry as is.

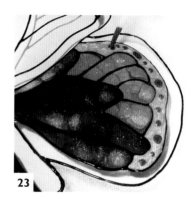

## E sections

*Chartreuse, lemon, and glitter medium*

Start on the right side (the left side is an identical mirror image).

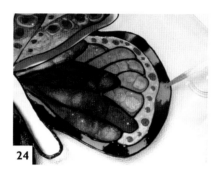

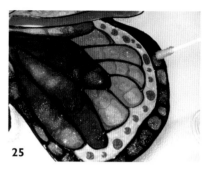

**24.** Fill in the section with chartreuse and lemon, alternating the two colors. Blend the paint with the tip of a toothpick.

**25.** Add drops of glitter medium, right next to each other, all the way around the section. Let dry as is.

## F sections

### Butterfly body

**26.** Pour a small amount of all the colors used in the project (except for the gold) into a small container and mix them together with a craft stick. The result will be a color that's almost black. Paint the body of the butterfly with this mixture. (If you have black paint, you can use it instead.)

### Remaining wing sections

**27.** Paint the two remaining wing sections with sky blue.

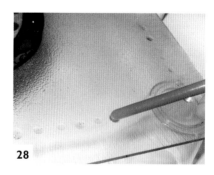

### Border finishing

**28.** Dip the end of a paintbrush handle into the glitter medium and use it to add dots of the medium all the way along the border between the frosted effect and the border. Let dry.

## Materials

**Pattern:** Page 148
**Surface:** Block of glass (with a hole in the base), available at stained glass shop

**Colors used:**
Cobalt blue, crimson, yellow, sand, apple green, super white

**Other products:**
Relief outliner: imitation lead

Glitter medium
Gloss gel medium

**Textures:**
Embossed effect, frosted effect

**Other materials:**
Black carbon paper
Stylus
Foam sponge block
Scissors
Palette
Small containers

## Preparing the piece

**1.** Clean the surface with rubbing alcohol and a paper towel.

## Transferring the pattern

Because the glass block is too thick to see the design through, you will need to transfer the pattern directly onto the block surface.

**2.** Place the pattern where you want it on the block and attach it with tape.

**3.** Slip the carbon paper underneath the pattern with the dark side down and use the stylus to transfer the design to the surface.

## Outlining the design

**4.** Cover the lines of the design, except for the outer edge, with relief outliner.

## Adding textures

**5.** Add the frosted effect (Y) and the embossed effect (X) in the sections indicated on the pattern. Let dry until the medium is completely clear.

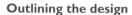

## Tip

For this project, it's best to use lights with LED bulbs, which will not get hot (a string of Christmas lights, for example, or a nightlight).

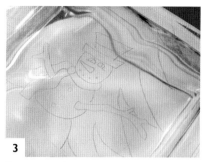

**3**

**4**

Pattern transferred onto the glass block

**5**

Y: Frosted effect

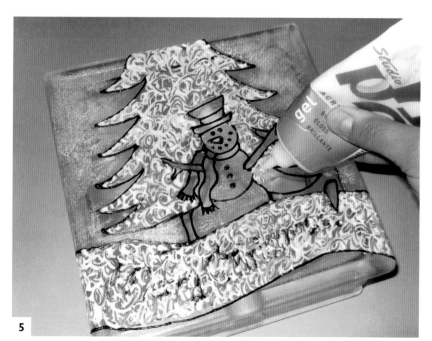

**5**

X: Embossed effect

### Painting

Paint the sections with the colors indicated (see below). Let the project dry for 24 hours, protected from dust.

### Pine tree

*Apple green with glitter medium*

**6.** In a small container, mix equal parts apple green and glitter medium.

**7.** Use a medium paintbrush to spread a thin coat of this mixture over the pine tree section. Let dry.

### Text banner

*Crimson with glitter medium*

**8.** In a small container, mix equal parts crimson and glitter medium.

**9.** Use a medium paintbrush to spread a thin coat of this mixture over the whole text banner section (you can also go over the relief outlined words if you wish).

**10.** Add drops of glitter medium here and there in the section to brighten up a few spots. Let dry.

### Snowman and other sections

**11.** Use toothpicks to fill in the following sections:

**Hat:** Crimson
**Hatband and scarf:** Blend of half cobalt blue and half glitter medium
**Snowman arms and tree trunk:** Sand
**Snowman nose and exclamation mark:** Yellow

### Border

**12.** Cut a square of sponge about ¾ inch on each side.

**13.** Pour a bit of yellow paint onto a palette (a paper plate works well) and dip the sponge in it. Blot the sponge on a clean portion of the palette to distribute the paint evenly over the sponge surface.

**14.** Use the sponge to spread paint over the outer edge of the block as evenly as possible. Don't go over the pine tree and the banner.

### Snowflakes

**15.** Dip the end of a paintbrush handle in super white paint and use it to add "snowflake" dots of different sizes over the whole project.

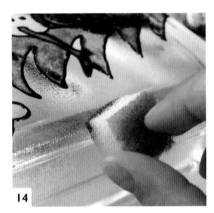

14

15

15

## Materials

**Pattern:** Page 149
**Surface:** Glass
**Size:** 16 x 20 in.

**Colors used:**
Sky blue, cobalt blue, crimson, yellow, purple, salmon, dark green, apple green, lavender

**Other products:**
Relief outliner: black
Glitter medium
Gloss gel medium

**Textures:**
Embossed effect, frosted effect, ripple effect, wave effect

**Other materials:**
Glazing resin or equivalent product
Stylus
Foam sponge
Scissors
Small scrap containers
Plastic knife

### Preparing the piece

**1.** Clean the glass with rubbing alcohol and a paper towel.

### Positioning the pattern

**2.** Place the pattern under the glass and attach it securely at the top and bottom with tape.

### Outlining the design

**3.** Cover all the lines of the design, except the outer edge and dashed lines, with relief outliner.

### Adding texture

There are a lot of textures to create in this project. Do them one at a time, following the instructions carefully. When each one is completed, let the gel medium dry completely before moving on to the next step.

## *Central section (oval)*

The central part is filled with two textures: a frosted effect (Y) and a wave effect (Z). Alternate between these two textures for all the sections (see pattern).

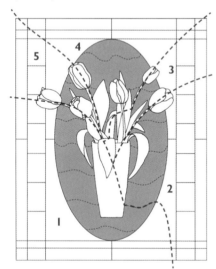

To fill in the center section, place the pattern underneath the glass again and use the dashed lines as a guide to where the sections begin and end. Because this is a large section to cover all at once, it's recommended that you do it in several parts (dashed red lines,

above) so that the medium doesn't dry before you're finished.

Prepare several squares of sponge in different sizes (for the frosted effect), a section of plastic knife blade (for the wave effect), and some cotton swabs before starting. You will need these tools at different points as you fill in the section. For this project, it's best to cut off the excess of the knife so that you only have about a half an inch left—there are a lot of small spaces to fill with texture and it will be easier to do them with a shortened knife.

**4.** Use a palette knife to spread a thin coat of gel medium over the whole section to the left of the flowers. The medium should not be too thin or you won't have time to work the texture before it dries (if the medium dries while you are working, apply it again).

**5.** As soon as the medium is applied, start to texture the sections. Begin by creating a frosted effect, dabbing the medium with the sponge, in the sections indicated (Y on the pattern), making sure not to go past the dashed lines.

**6.** Next, fill in the other sections (Z) with the wave effect, again making sure to stay within the lines.

> **Important:** While adding the textures, slide a piece of colored paper between the pattern and the glass from time to time to see if the texture is uniform.

**7.** As soon as the textures are finished in this left section, moisten a cotton swab with water and wipe off the medium along the inside edge of the oval and along each of the dashed lines, creating a clear space the width of a swab. The borders must be clear and well defined as they will be prominent once the medium has dried.

**8.** Repeat these steps for the rest of the sections. Let dry completely, until the medium is completely clear.

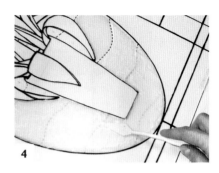

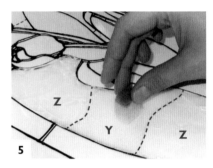

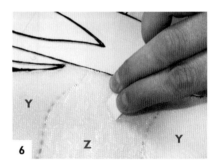

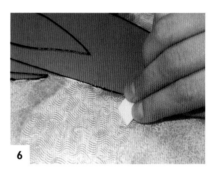

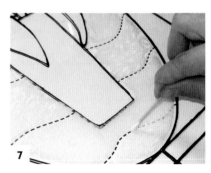

See page 26 for a photo showing the finished textures.

## Vase, inner and outer frame sections

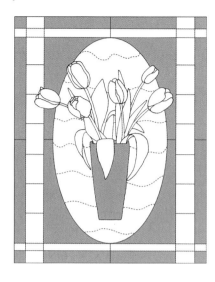

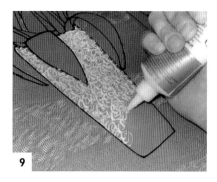

**9.** Create an embossed effect in all the shaded sections (see the diagram at left).

## Columns

The columns are worked in two steps—there are two textures to create, one on top of the other.

**10.** Create a ripple effect in all the shaded sections (see diagram). Let dry until the medium is clear.

**11.** Once the first texture is completely dry, create a frosted effect in all the same sections.

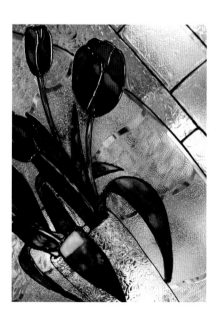

Do this step one section at a time: As soon as you finish applying the medium with the sponge, wipe off the gel along the inside edge of the section with a clean cotton swab. You will create a clearer border once the medium has dried.

When all the sections are filled in and completely dry, go on to the next step.

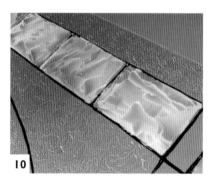

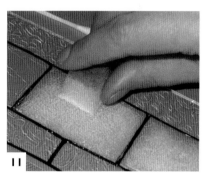

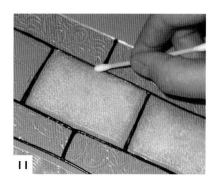

## Painting

Paint the following sections with the colors indicated in the pattern. Let dry for 24 hours before going on to the final step.

### Greenery and flower stems

*Dark green (V), apple green (G), and lightening medium*

All the leaves are painted in the same way. Do them one at a time, because you need to create a base of different colors in each one. On the diagram, the dotted lines indicate where the colors meet. For the small sections with just one color, simply fill them in with a toothpick.

**12.** Use a paintbrush to paint a leaf with the two base colors: apple green and dark green. The two colors must touch. Then wipe the paintbrush off with a paper towel to remove the excess paint

**13.** Next, dip a clean cotton swab in lightening medium and add a few drops to the section.

**14.** Use the tip of the cleaned paintbrush to gently blend the three products and create subtle shading in the leaf.

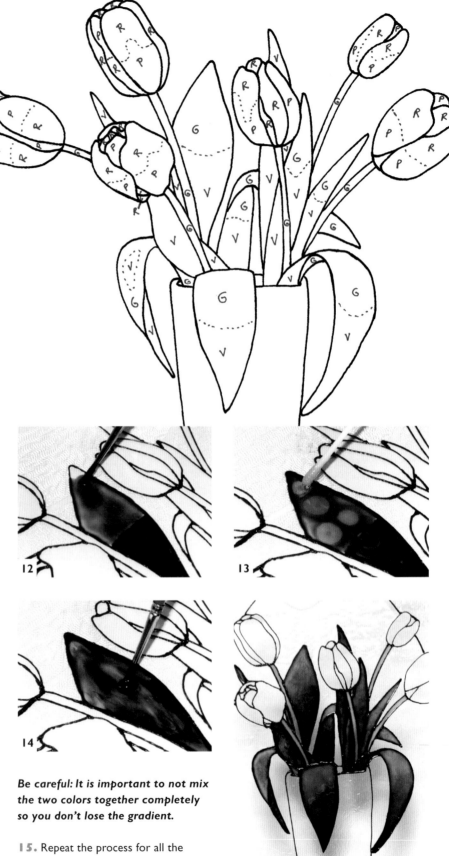

*Be careful: It is important to not mix the two colors together completely so you don't lose the gradient.*

**15.** Repeat the process for all the leaves in the bouquet.

## Red tulips

*Purple (P), crimson (R), and lightening medium*

**16.** All the tulips are painted in the same as the leaves; only the colors are different. I recommend that you do the sections one at a time, since you have to create a gradient in each one. In the diagram (page 82), the dashed lines indicate where the sections of color meet. For the small sections with just one color, simply fill them in with a toothpick.

16

Adding the base colors

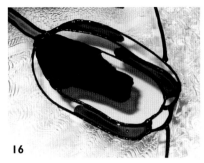

16

Example of the position of the purple in one flower

## Vase and other sections

*Various colors*

The vase is painted in two steps.

**17.** Use a paintbrush to apply a thin coat of parma over the whole section. Let dry for 24 hours.

**18.** The next day, apply a uniform coat of purple over the parma. Note: the parma base coat will give the purple added richness and depth.

**19.** Paint all the sections with the colors indicated in the pattern (see key at right). Use toothpicks for the small sections and a paintbrush for the larger ones. For the textured sections, you'll need to use a paintbrush, since you have to spread the paint in a thin coat.

**20.** Let dry for 24 hours, protected from dust. Finally, go on to the last step.

**Color key**

(see the pattern)

**B** = Sky blue
**V** = Apple green
**S** = Salmon
**J** = Blend of half yellow and half lightening medium
**R** = Crimson
**C** = Cobalt blue

17

Applying the parma (first step)

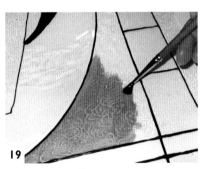

19

A thin coat over the texture

19

Adding cobalt blue over the texture

19

Filling in sections with salmon

## Finishing touches

Complete the project by adding the following details.

### Decorative flourishes

**21.** Place the pattern back under the glass.

**22.** Use gloss gel medium to add the decorative flourishes (the dashed lines on the pattern) found in the two columns.

22

### Decorative dots

(center section only)

The decorative dots are made with glazing resin. Follow the manufacturer's instructions to prepare the product. You don't need much for this project; a few drops should be plenty.

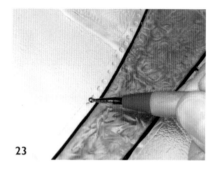

23

24

**23.** Once your product is prepared, dip a stylus in the mixture and use it to apply tiny dots along the middle of all the clear lines in the central section.

**24.** Let dry for 24 hours or until the resin solidifies completely.

*You can also make these dots using lightening medium—although, in this case, the dots won't be as raised or as clear as with resin, and they will have a slightly yellow tint.*

## Materials

**Pattern:** Page 150
**Surface:** Glass
**Measurements:** 8 x 10 in.

**Colors used:**
Lemon, crimson, orange,
apple green, old pink

**Other products:**
Gloss gel medium

**Textures:**
Frosted effect
Ripple effect

**Other materials:**
Palette knife
Masking tape

This project can be displayed in any orientation you like.

## Preparing the piece

1. Clean the glass with rubbing alcohol and a paper towel.

## Positioning the pattern

2. Place the pattern under the glass and attach it securely at the top and bottom with tape.

## Creating the clear lines

3. Cover all the lines with masking tape, centering the tape over the lines. It is important to make sure there is a good seal between the tape and glass along the tape's entire length.

## Creating the tiles

4. Use a palette knife to apply a uniform coat of gel medium across the whole surface in preparation for creating the ripple effect. The coat of medium should be of a uniform medium thickness and not have large peaks.

5. As soon as the surface is covered with the medium, carefully remove the masking tape. This process is fairly delicate, since you have to remove all the masking tape at the same time, before the medium dries.

6. Finally, retouch any imperfections as needed and let dry until the medium becomes clear.

### A good idea!

This project is unique because it does not require relief outliner or adhesive lead strip. You can have fun with this technique and create tiles of all sizes with just masking tape.

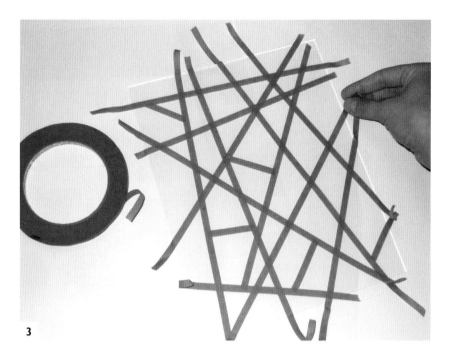

3

4

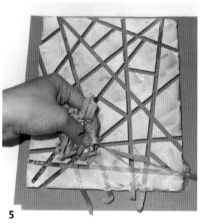

5

6

## Painting

**7.** Paint all the sections with the colors indicated (see the key). Use a paintbrush, as you need to spread the paint in a thin coat, as uniform as possible, over the textured sections. If you go outside the section, quickly wipe up the paint with a cotton swab.

### Color key

(see the pattern)

**V** = Apple green
**O** = Orange
**J** = Lemon
**C** = Crimson
**R** = Old pink

Decorative dots in the clear borders: Apple green

**8.** Adding the decorative dots in the clear borders is optional. They can be added anywhere you like. To make them, just dip the tip of a paintbrush handle in the apple green paint and use it to create a series of five dots in a row.

**9.** Let dry for 24 hours before going on to the last step.

## Finishing touch

*Gloss gel medium*

**10.** Once all the paint is completely dry, all you have left to do is to create the frosted effect on the clear sections between the colored tiles. Use a piece of sponge slightly narrower than the masking tape, and wipe off any medium that gets on the tiles. Let the medium dry completely.

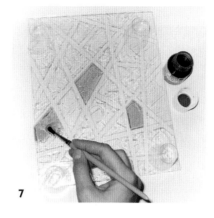

7

7

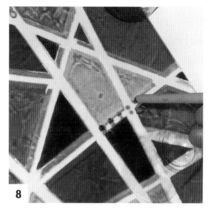

8

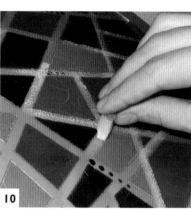

10

The project before creating a frosted effect.

## 12

Art deco panel

## Materials

**Pattern:** Page 151
**Surface:** Glass
**Measurements:** 8 x 10 in.

**Colors used:**
Turquoise blue, salmon,
apple green, red-violet

**Other products:**
Relief outliner: black
Gloss gel medium
Pearlescent medium

**Texture:**
Embossed effect

**Other materials:**
Small containers
Large toothpicks

## Preparing the piece

**1.** Clean the glass with rubbing alcohol and a paper towel.

## Positioning the pattern

**2.** Place the pattern under the glass and attach it securely at the top and bottom with tape.

## Outlining the design

**3.** Cover all the lines of the design, except the dashed lines on the pattern, with relief outliner.

## Adding texture

**4.** Create an embossed effect in all the sections marked with an X on the pattern.

**5.** Let dry until the gel medium becomes completely transparent. Then go on to the painting step.

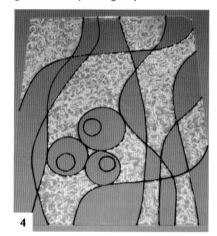

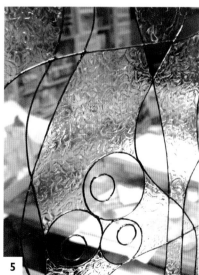

**5**

Dry embossed effect

## Painting

**6.** Prepare the color blends one at a time in small containers and paint all the sections indicated on the pattern (with an R, M, B, or V; see the key below). Once you finish with one blend, go on to the next. If you accidentally paint the outline, wipe the paint off quickly with a paper towel before it dries.

**7.** Once all the sections are filled in, let dry for 24 hours, protected from dust.

*Important: To get good results with a pearly color, you must use a very thick coat of paint and check often against a light to make sure it is distributed evenly throughout the section—you will see clear spots where there is not enough paint.*

*I recommend that you use a paintbrush for these sections, in order to work more quickly. As well, you can use the brush to create a uniform look in the pearly paint by gently tapping the surface while moving the brush in little twists.*

**6**

Applying blend R

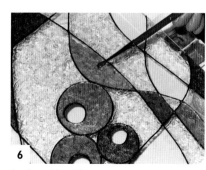

**6**

Applying blend V

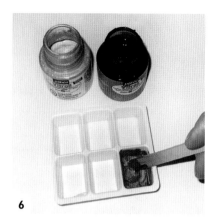

**6**

### Note

Pearlescent colors are not very attractive when backlit. They look fantastic, however, against an opaque background, light or dark. This faux stained glass panel is perfect for the door of a cabinet or other furniture that is not lit from inside.

Another suggestion: You can also paint the textured sections with a dark, transparent color of your choice if you don't want what's behind the panel to be visible.

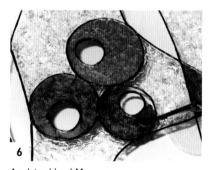

**6**

Applying blend M

### Color key

(see the pattern)

**R** = Half salmon and half pearlescent medium
**M** = Half red-violet and half pearlescent medium
**B** = Half turquoise and half pearlescent medium
**V** = Half apple green and half pearlescent medium

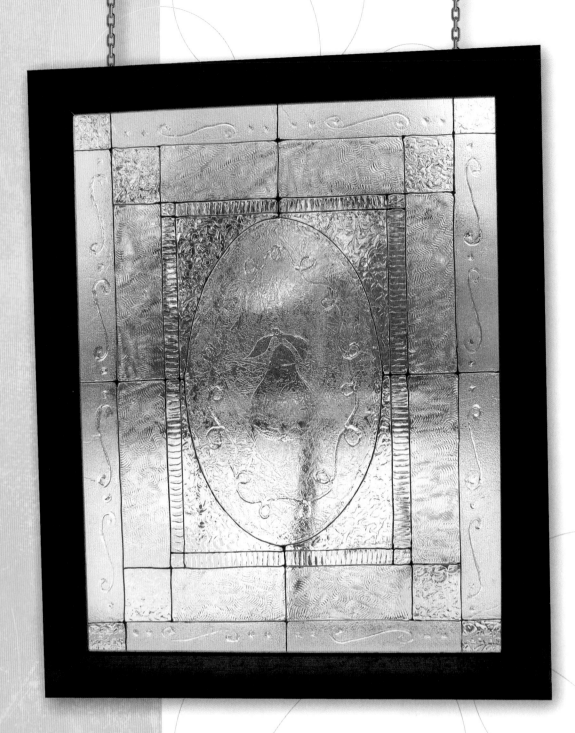

## 13

## Materials

**Pattern:** Page 152
**Surface:** Glass
**Measurements:** 11 x 14 in.

**Other products:**
Relief outliner: gold
Pearlescent medium
Gloss gel medium

**No colors!**

**Textures:**
Marbled effect, ripple effect, wave effect, stencil effect, frosted effect, embossed effect, contour effect

**Other materials:**
Stencil of your choice (the motif must be smaller than the section inside the central vine)

This faux stained-glass window is made using only gloss gel medium, without color. Several different textures fill the different sections, with a stenciled design in the very center. For this part, it's up to you to pick your favorite stencil design.

Stencils are sold at most art and craft stores.

## Preparing the piece

**1.** Clean the glass with rubbing alcohol and a paper towel.

## Positioning the pattern

**2.** Place the pattern under the glass and attach it securely at the top and bottom with tape.

## Outlining the design

**3.** Cover the lines of the design—except the outside edge and the dashed lines—with the gold relief outliner.

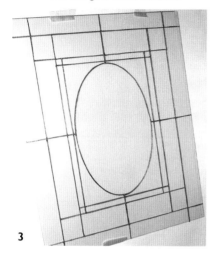

3

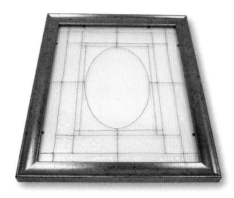

## Adding texture

**4.** Add texture to the different sections of the piece, following the order shown below. It's important to follow the order given, as certain textures are applied on top of others. Remember that the underlying layers must be completely dry before new ones are added.

Refer to the chapter on textures (page 28) for how to create them and to the diagrams below for where to place them. Once you've finished creating the textures, let them dry until the gel medium becomes transparent.

## Create the textures in this order:

1—Marbled effect

2—Ripple effect

3—Wave effect

4—Stencil effect (your stencil design must fit inside the central flourish)

5—Frosted effect (on top of the textured effect)

6—Embossed effect

7—Simply add short lines of gel medium throughout the section

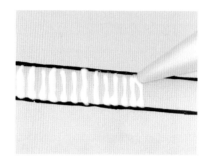

8—Contour effect (the last thing to do) After tracing the outlines of all the sections indicated in gray, go over all the dashed lines (decorative flourishes and dots) on the design. Place the pattern back underneath the glass if it's been removed.

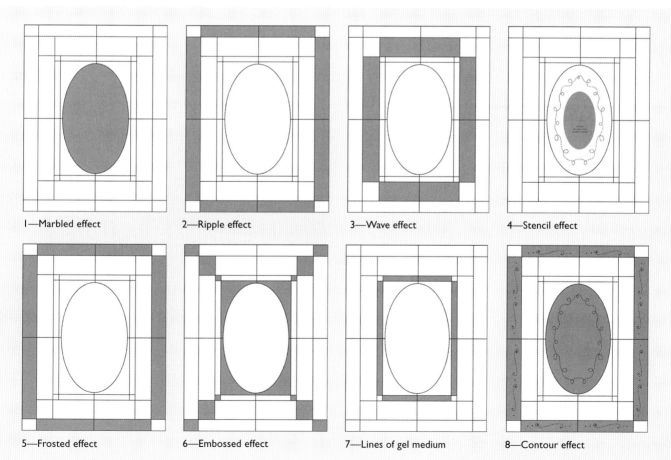

1—Marbled effect    2—Ripple effect    3—Wave effect    4—Stencil effect

5—Frosted effect    6—Embossed effect    7—Lines of gel medium    8—Contour effect

## Materials

**Pattern:** Page 153
**Surface:** Glass
**Measurements (glass):**
9½ x 4½ in.
**Measurements (box):**
12 x 6¾ x 3 in.

**Colors used:**
Black, apple green, blue
jeans, red

**Other products:**
Relief outliner: black
Pearlescent medium

**Other materials:**
Fine paintbrush (to retouch
  the black)
Small scrap containers
Stylus

## Preparing the piece

**1.** Clean the glass with rubbing alcohol and a paper towel.

## Positioning the pattern

**2.** Place the pattern under the glass and attach it securely at the top and bottom with tape.

## Outlining the design

**3.** Cover the lines of the design, except the outside edge, with the relief outliner. Note that the lettering must be entirely filled in with the relief outliner.

## Painting

Paint the sections with the colors indicated (see the pattern). Let dry for 24 hours before moving on to the final step.

### *Section A*

*Pearlescent medium and apple green*

**4.** Mix equal amounts of apple green and pearlescent medium in a small container. You'll need enough paint to completely fill in the center section.

**5.** Use a medium-sized paintbrush to paint section A; this will make things go much faster. It is important to not spread the paint too thinly. To obtain a beautiful result with a pearly color, you need to apply a very thick coat of paint, gently tapping the surface with the paintbrush throughout to achieve a uniform look.

**6.** The closer you get to the lettering, the more careful you need to be to not go over the words; using a toothpick will help with this.

**7.** Once the section is filled in, use a clean cotton swab to wipe off any paint that got on the relief outliner. (If some of the paint won't come off, it's not a big problem—you'll retouch the black sections in the next step.)

A small plastic container holds the mixture.

**4**

**5**

**6**

**7**

### R Sections

*Red*

**8.** Use a paintbrush to fill in all the R sections with the red paint.

### B Sections

*Blue jeans*

**9.** Use a paintbrush to fill in all the B sections with the blue jeans paint.

### Finishing touches

When all the paint in the large sections is completely dry, add the finishing touches described below. Then let the project dry another 24 hours or until the paint is completely dry and hard to the touch. Finally, insert your painted panel into the top of the box (which you have already painted however you like).

### Retouch the black sections

**10.** Use a fine paintbrush with a stiff tip to delicately retouch the lettering and redefine its outline with the black paint.

**11.** Dip the tip of the handle of your paintbrush into the black paint and use it to add a dot in each of the four corners of section A.

### Small green dots

**12.** In another small container, mix up a half-and-half blend of pearlescent medium and apple green. Dip a stylus in this blend and make little dots all along the edges of the R and B sections, creating a frame for the central section.

### Tip

It's best to use opaque colors for this kind of project, as the light won't go through. This way, the lid of your box will hide what's inside—which won't be the case if you use transparent colors.

# So many possibilities!

This project is worked on the door of a wardrobe in order to subtly hide its contents. The same design can also be worked on a pane of glass or plexiglass separating two rooms in a house. You can place two copies of this design together to get a different size and shape. This design can also be used on a long mirror to add a dash of style to your decor (transfer the design to the surface in this case).

## Materials

**Pattern:** Pages 154 and 155
**Surface:** Glass
**Measurements:** 9 x 51 in.

**Colors used:**
White, green-gold, purple, super white

**Other products:**
Relief outliner: vermeil gold
Gloss gel medium

**Textures:**
Embossed effect, frosted effect

## Preparing the piece

**1.** Clean the glass with rubbing alcohol and a paper towel.

## Positioning the pattern

**2.** Place the pattern under the glass and attach it securely at the top and bottom with tape.

## Outlining the design

**3.** Cover all the lines of the design—except the outside edge and the dashed lines—with the relief outliner.

## Adding texture

**4.** Create an embossed effect (X) and a frosted effect (Y) in the sections indicated on the pattern, although the embossed effect doesn't actually require an additional step (see the explanation below). Once the textures are completed, let dry until the gel medium becomes transparent. Then go on to the painting step.

## *Embossed effect*

You will create a frosted border around the edge at the same time as you create the embossed effect, doing one section at a time.

**5.** Start by creating the embossed effect throughout the whole section.

**6.** As soon as the section is filled in, pat the medium along the outer edge of the design with a square of sponge about half an inch wide to create a frosted effect (the dotted lines in the pattern indicate the width of this border). Don't pat the texture in the whole section—only along the outer edge. The goal is to create a uniform border all the way around the glass panel.

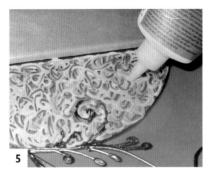

5

Embossed effect

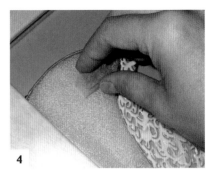

4

Frosted effect

6

Adding a frosted border

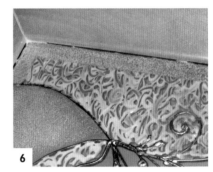

6

Completed texturing

The textures as they dry

## Painting

Paint all the following elements with the colors indicated using toothpicks. Quickly clean up any paint that gets on the relief outliner. Once the sections are painted, let dry for 24 hours, protected from dust.

### Leaves

*Green-gold and white*

All the leaves are filled in using the same method. Work them one at a time, as you have to create a foundation of mixed colors in each one.

8

9

**7.** Fill in the first leaf with the green-gold paint.

**8.** Dip a clean toothpick in the white paint and let a drop of paint fall onto the base of the leaf.

**9.** With the tip of the toothpick, gently blend the two colors to create subtle variations within the leaf. Repeat this process for all the leaves, varying the tints.

### Tulips

*Purple and white*

**10.** Follow the same method as for the leaves, using purple instead of green-gold for the base color. Fill in the tulips one at a time, since you have to create color variations within each one.

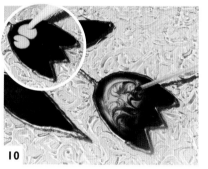

10

Blending the colors

10

The result

### Adapting patterns to different dimensions

You can join several patterns side by side to get a design with different dimensions. Repeat as many copies of the pattern as necessary, in mirror image, to achieve the desired width.

*Be careful: Create the frosted border only around the outer edge of a combined design like this (as indicated in red).*

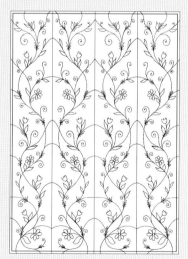

White sections, pattern p. 154
Yellow sections, pattern p. 155

### White flowers

Super white

**11.** Simply fill in all the sections of the flowers with the super white paint.

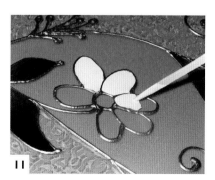

11

This pretty plaque can decorate a front door or a door to a bedroom or a room in a retirement community or nursing home.

You can replace the text with the name of the person the room or house belongs to, if you wish.

## Materials

**Pattern:** Page 156
**Surface:** Wood
**Measurements:**
9³/₄ x 6³/₄ in.

**Colors used:**
Sky blue, apple green, sun yellow, red, super white, black

**Other products:**
Relief outliner: black
Lightening medium
Glitter medium
Gesso and a flat paintbrush
Acrylic varnish (matte or gloss)

**Other materials:**
Black carbon paper and stylus
Eraser

## Preparing the piece

The wooden plaque must be well sanded and smooth to the touch.

**1.** Apply gesso over the surface with a flat paintbrush (adding a second coat, as needed). The paint must be opaque and hide the grain of the wood. Let dry.

**2.** Next, apply a coat of acrylic varnish or an all-purpose sealant over the surface to seal it even more. Let dry.

## Transferring the pattern

**3.** Place the pattern in position and attach it at the top with tape. Insert a sheet of black carbon paper dark side down underneath the pattern and transfer the design to the surface with a stylus.

## Outlining the design

**4.** Cover all the lines of the design, except the outside edge, with the relief outliner. Let dry. Erase any lines of the design that are still visible.

## Painting

Paint each of the sections as instructed. Let dry for 24 hours before going on to the final step.

### Center background (A)

The background is worked in two steps—don't let it dry in between steps.

**5.** Use a paintbrush to fill in the whole background (A) with the sky blue paint. Work quickly and apply enough paint to obtain a smooth, shiny finish.

**6.** Once the background is painted, dip a cotton swab in the glitter medium and use it to add small drops of the medium throughout the background, varying the sizes of the drops. Let dry as is.

7

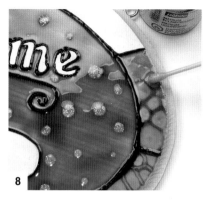

8

### Border (B)

The border sections are worked in two steps—don't let them dry between steps.

**7.** Use a paintbrush to quickly fill in the sections with the apple green paint.

**8.** As soon as the sections are filled in, dip a cotton swab in the lightening medium and add drops of it on the section, right next to each other. Let dry as is.

### Bee

**9.** Fill in the sections of the bee as follows:
**Body of the bee (N):** Black
**Head and other body sections:** Sun yellow
**Wings:** Super white

### The lettering

**10.** Use a toothpick to paint the words with the red paint.

10

### Finishing touches

**11.** Finish the project with these last touches. Let dry completely (24 hours).

**Wings:** With a gentle touch, add a little swirl of relief outliner in the center of each wing.
**Dotted border:** Dip a stylus in the super white paint and add a line of little dots around the edge of the central section.
**Side edges:** Paint the edges of the plaque with the black paint or another color of your choice.

11

Decorative plaque—Frog

## Materials

**Pattern:** Page 157
**Surface:** Wood
**Measurements:**
9¾ x 6¾ in.

**Colors used:**
Turquoise blue, black, orange, pink, blue jeans, wheat yellow, red, light green

**Other products:**
Relief outliner: black
Lightening medium
Glitter medium
Gesso and a flat paintbrush
Green and black acrylic paint (for the border)
Acrylic varnish (matte or gloss)

**Other materials:**
Black carbon paper and stylus
Eraser
Plastic "googly" eyes
Pliers
Small container

## Preparing the piece

First, make sure the wooden plaque is well sanded and smooth to the touch.

**1.** Apply one or two coats of gesso over the surface with the flat paint-brush, as needed. The gesso must be opaque and hide the grain of the wood. Let dry.

**2.** Next, apply a coat of acrylic varnish or an all-purpose sealant over the surface to seal it even more. Let dry.

## Transferring the pattern

**3.** Place the pattern in position and attach it at the top with tape. Insert a sheet of black carbon paper dark side down underneath the pattern and transfer the design to the surface with a stylus.

*Don't trace the eyes if you want to use plastic eyes on your frog.*

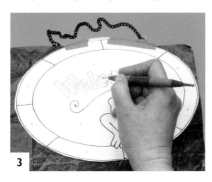

3

3

## Outlining the design

**4.** Cover all the lines of the design, except the outside edge, with the relief outliner. Let dry, then erase any lines of the design that are still visible.

5

## Painting

Paint each of the sections as instructed below. Let dry for 24 hours.

### Frog (A)

*Light green with plastic eyes*

**5.** First, paint the frog with the light green paint.

As soon as you've finished painting, place the two eyes in position, directly on the wet paint (without getting paint on the fronts of the eyes). Let dry.

**6.** Next, use a toothpick to fill in the other sections of the frog as follows:
**Tongue:** Pink
**Inside of the mouth:** Black

7

5

### Border (C)

*Turquoise blue and lightening medium*

The border sections (C) are worked in two steps; do each section one at a time.

**7.** Start by filling in the section with the turquoise blue paint. It's best to use a paintbrush for this part so you can work quickly.

**8.** Dip a cotton swab in the lightening medium and add some drops of the medium right next to each other throughout the section. Let dry as is.

**9.** Repeat these two steps for each of the border sections, varying the size of the drops.

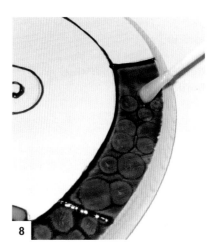

8

## Central background (B)

*Orange, red, glitter medium, and lightening medium*

The background is painted in three steps.

**10.** Use a paintbrush to quickly fill in the whole background with the red and then the orange paint. Use enough paint to create a smooth and shiny finish.

**11.** Once the background is painted, add a few drops of glitter medium to it to give it a bit of sparkle. Blend the medium gently into the colors with a paintbrush.

**12.** Immediately afterward, dip a cotton swab into the lightening medium and add small drops throughout the background, varying the size of the drops. Let dry as is.

## The lettering

*Black*

**13.** Use a toothpick to fill in the letters with the black paint. Let these dry completely before moving on to the final steps.

......................................

## Finishing touches

Once all the sections are completely dry, add the finishing touches.

## Decorative dots

**14.** Dip a stylus in the paint and add small dots of color in the following sections:
**Frog:** red, wheat yellow, blue jeans
**Central background:** wheat yellow
**Border:** red

## Edge of the plaque

**15.** The side edge of the plaque is simply painted with green acrylic paint, the same shade as the frog.

12

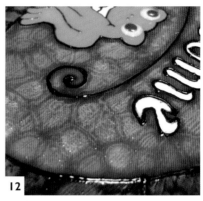

12

Result.

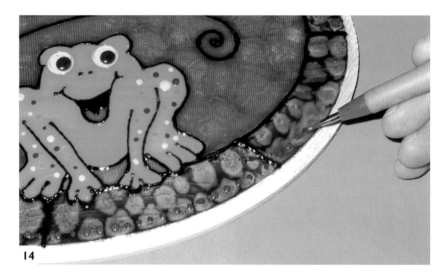

14

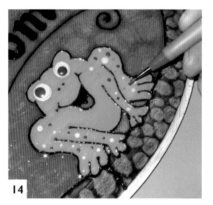

14

15

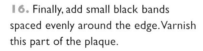

16

**16.** Finally, add small black bands spaced evenly around the edge. Varnish this part of the plaque.

## Materials

**Pattern:** Page 158
**Surface:** Wood
**Measurements:**
9¾ x 6¾ in.

**Colors used:**
wheat yellow, red,
clementine, sun yellow, blue
jeans

**Other products:**
Relief outliner: black
Acrylic paint: brown and
cream
Acrylic varnish (matte or
gloss)

**Other materials:**
Black carbon paper and
stylus
Eraser
Medium-size flat paintbrush
for acrylic paints
Small container

This pretty plaque highlights the beauty of the wood's grain. Since there is no white base under the colors, it's important to use a pale wood (such as pine or poplar) without any knots.

You can also replace the large sunflower with a house number.

## Preparing the piece

The wooden plaque must be well sanded and smooth to the touch.

### Staining the background

1. In a small container, mix one part brown acrylic paint with four parts water. The total amount of the mixture must be enough to cover the surface of the plaque. You can modify this blend if you want a lighter or darker background.

2. Spread the mixture across the whole surface with a flat paintbrush, brushing with the grain of the wood.

3. Use a paper towel to wipe away excess paint and let dry.

4. Finally, apply a coat of acrylic varnish or all-purpose sealant on the plaque to seal it further. Let dry.

### Transferring the pattern

5. Place the pattern in position on the piece and attach it at the top with

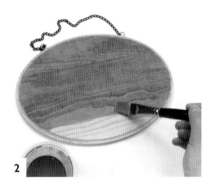

2

3

tape. Place the carbon paper under the pattern with the dark side down and transfer the design to the surface with a stylus.

### Outlining the design

6. Cover all the lines of the design, except the outside edge, with the relief outliner. Let dry, then erase any lines from the carbon paper that are still visible.

5

It isn't absolutely necessary to apply varnish or sealant to the wood. It all depends on whether the wood is very porous and whether or not you want a shiny finish.

### Painting

7. Paint all the sections of the project. Let dry for 24 hours before moving on to the final step.

Use toothpicks to fill in the smaller sections and a paintbrush for the larger ones.

**Sunflower petals:** wheat yellow
**Sunflower centers:** sun yellow
**Lettering:** red
**Border (A):** blue jeans
**Small decorative dots:** clementine, plus a few in blue jeans

### Finishing touches

### Varnishing

8. Apply a coat of lightening medium over the stained wood (after it's dry) to give it a shiny look.

7

7

8

### Edge of the plaque

9. Finally, paint the border of the plaque with acrylic paint in the color of your choice (here, cream), then varnish it. *Note that you could also paint the border with a glass paint of your choice.*

## 19

## Materials

**Pattern:** Page 159
**Surface:** Framed mirror
**Measurements:** 11 x 14 in.

**Colors used:**
Cobalt blue, lemon, crimson, apple green, purple

**Other products:**
Relief outliner: vermeil gold
Glitter medium
Gloss gel medium

**Texture:**
Embossed effect

**Other materials:**
Small container
Black carbon paper and stylus
Small and large toothpicks
Ruler

## Preparing the piece

**1.** Clean the surface with rubbing alcohol and a paper towel.

## Transferring the pattern

**2.** Place the pattern on the surface and attach it securely at the top with tape.

**3.** Use the carbon paper and stylus to transfer all the lines of the design to the surface. Use a ruler for the straight lines.

## Outlining the design

**4.** Cover all the lines of the design with the relief outliner. If you are working on a framed mirror, put a line along the outside edge of the mirror as well (where it meets the frame) to keep the paint from running onto the frame. Let dry, then use a cotton swab to erase any lines from the carbon paper that are still visible.

## Adding texture

**5.** Create the embossed texture in all the shaded sections as shown on the diagram. Let dry until the medium is completely clear, then go on to the painting step.

5

Some sections of this design are not painted in order to emphasize the texture. But you can certainly paint them as well if you prefer.

Dry embossed effect texture

## Painting

**6.** Paint all the sections with the colors indicated (see the key). Use toothpicks for the small sections and a paintbrush for the larger ones. Use the paintbrush for all the textured sections, as you must spread the paint over these sections in a thin coat. The greenery and the tulips are worked differently and are described below.

Let the project dry for 24 hours, protected from dust.

### Color key

(see the pattern)

**B** = Cobalt blue
**J** = Lemon
**C** = Crimson
**V** = Apple green
**P** = Blend of half purple and half glitter medium

## Greenery

*Apple green and glitter medium*

**7.** Use a small toothpick to fill in all the sections of greenery with the apple green paint.

**8.** Add a dab of glitter medium to each of these sections.

**9.** Finally, blend each section with a toothpick to create a bright, sparkly green.

## Tulips

*Crimson and glitter medium*

**10.** Paint the tulips using the same method as the greenery, using crimson as the base color instead of apple green.

Don't go outside the lines when you are filling in the sections. If you accidentally do, quickly wipe up the excess paint.

**6**

Filling in a section with lemon

**6**

Painting a textured section with crimson

**8**

**9**

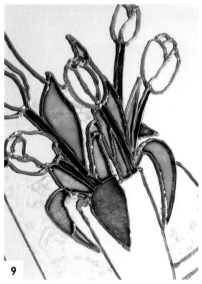

**9**

Finished greenery sections

**10**

## 20

*Kitten mirror*

## Materials

**Pattern:** Page 160
**Surface:** Mirror
**Measurements:** 16 x 20 in.

**Colors used:**
Turquoise blue, black, orange, parma, apple green

**Other products:**
Relief outliner: vermeil gold
Glitter medium
Gloss gel medium

**Texture:**
Embossed effect

**Other materials:**
Small containers
Black carbon paper and stylus
Ruler

## Preparing the piece

**1.** Clean the surface with rubbing alcohol and a paper towel.

## Transferring the pattern

**2.** Place the pattern on the surface and attach it securely at the top with tape. Use the carbon paper and stylus to transfer all the lines of the pattern to the mirror. Use the ruler for the straight lines.

## Outlining the design

**3.** Go over all the lines of the design with the relief outliner. If you are working on a framed mirror, put a line along the outside edge of the mirror as well (where it meets the frame) to keep the paint from running onto the frame.

**4.** Let dry completely, then use a cotton swab to erase any lines from the carbon paper that are still visible.

## Adding texture

**5.** Create the embossed effect in all the shaded sections as shown on the diagram. Let dry until the medium becomes clear, then go on to the painting step.

## Painting

**6.** Paint all the sections with the colors indicated on the pattern and color key.

Use toothpicks for the small sections and a paintbrush for the larger ones. Use the paintbrush for all the textured sections, since you must spread the paint over these sections in a thin coat.

Don't go outside the relief outliner lines. If you accidentally do, wipe up the excess paint immediately.

**7.** Let dry for 24 hours in a dry place, protected from dust.

## Variation

Have fun changing up the colors! The cat could be black, white, brown, or even gray if you want.

## Color key

(see the pattern)

**O** = Blend of half orange and half glitter medium
**B** = Blend of half turquoise and half glitter medium
**V** = Apple green
**N** = Black
**P** = Parma
**Nose and inside ears** = Black
**Bell** = Glitter medium

## 21

# Peace tortoise

A three-
dimensional
project

## Materials

**Pattern:** Page 161
**Surface:** Wooden tortoise
(something similar might be
available online, or at a craft
or hobby store)
**Measurements:** 7 x 9 x 3
in. approx.

**Colors used:**
Cobalt blue, crimson,
emerald, yellow, parma,
apple green

**Other products:**
Relief outliner: black and
gold

Glitter medium
Gloss gel medium
Gesso
Acrylic paint: brick red,
black
Acrylic varnish (satin or
gloss finish)

**Other materials:**
Small container
Palette knife
Black carbon paper and
stylus
Flat medium-size paintbrush
for acrylic paint

## Preparing the piece

*The wooden tortoise must be well sanded and smooth to the touch.*

**1.** Apply gesso over the shell with the flat paintbrush, using two coats, if needed. The paint must be opaque and hide the grain of the wood. Let dry before going on to the next step.

## Transferring the pattern

**2.** Center the pattern on the shell and attach it in several places with tape, cutting slits into it as needed in order to fit the pattern smoothly over the rounded shell.

**3.** Slide the carbon paper underneath the pattern with the dark side down and use the stylus to transfer the design to the surface.

**4.** Remove the pattern and carbon paper and use a lead pencil to draw a wavy line all the way around the edge of the shell, about half an inch from the edge.

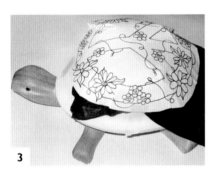

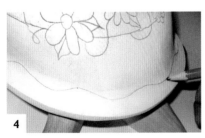

## Adding a base texture

**5.** Using a palette knife, apply a coat of gloss gel medium over the whole shell to create a textured effect. The texture should be even and without large peaks. Let dry until the medium becomes clear, then go on to the next step.

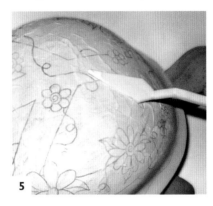

## Outlining the design

**6.** Cover all the lines of the design with the black relief outliner. Let dry completely.

## Painting

**7.** Paint all the sections described in the color key, along with the shell background, with the colors indicated (the shell background is described in detail on the next page). Once these sections are filled in, let the piece dry for 24 hours before going on to the final steps.

*Important: When you are painting on a three-dimensional piece, it's essential to not use too much paint. Since this paint is very fluid and you are painting on an angled surface, you should apply the paint in a very thin coat, and use multiple coats to achieve the desired shade of color. Let the paint dry in between coats for at least four to six hours.*

## Color key

**Peace sign:** Blend of half cobalt blue and half glitter medium
**Leaves:** Apple green
**Border along bottom edge:** Yellow
**Flower 1:** Parma
**Center:** Crimson

**Flower 2:** Crimson
**Center:** Yellow

**Flower 3:** Yellow
**Center:** Crimson

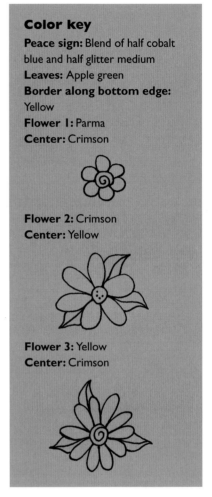

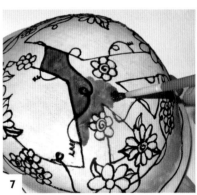

## Tip

You can use this pattern on any three-dimensional wood piece.

## Shell background

*Emerald and apple green*

The background of the shell is different from the other sections—it's worked in two steps.

**8.** Start by spreading a coat of emerald paint over all the background sections. Let the paint set for about 15 to 30 minutes or until it's sticky to the touch.

**9.** Next, dip a cotton swab in solvent, blotting it on a paper towel to remove any excess. Gently rub the paint to lighten certain parts and allow the wood texture to show through.

Change cotton swabs as often as needed, as they will rapidly fill with paint. If you rub too hard and take off all the paint, just paint over the spot with a little more emerald paint. Let dry for 24 hours.

**10.** Once the base layer is completely dry, spread a coat of apple green over these same sections to change the shade of the background. Let dry.

**Finishing touches**

*Decorative dots*

**11.** Dip the end of a paintbrush handle in the cobalt blue paint and add little dots all the way around the yellow border.

*Edge of the yellow border*

**12.** Add little stripes of crimson about half an inch wide around the edge of the yellow border.

**Tracing the outlines with gold**

**13.** Go over all the lines of the design again with gold relief outliner for a stylish finish.

*Body of the tortoise*

**14.** The legs and head of the tortoise are simply painted with acrylic paint: brick red for the head and legs and

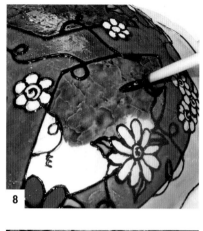

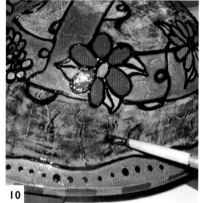
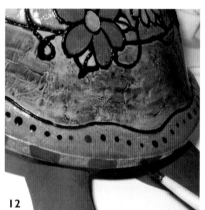

black for the ends of the legs and tail. Apply a coat of satin or gloss varnish over these parts to protect the paint.

## 22

*Marbling technique*

## Materials

**No pattern**
**Surface of your choice:**
glass plate, canvas, vase,
pane of glass

**Colors used:**
All your favorites!

**Other materials:**
Large pan (big enough to
    dip the piece into)
Cotton swabs, craft sticks
Rubber gloves

This technique is creative and fun. You
can use it on all kinds of surfaces, such
as a canvas, vase, piece of metal, even
a window pane. Each piece created
will be unique, and the possibilities are
limitless.

## Preparing the pan

**1.** The pan must be larger than the piece you are decorating. You can use an aluminum pan, large bowl, tray, or a disposable plastic container. Fill the container with enough water to dip the piece into, at least two inches deep. Prepare a piece of cardboard or plastic to set the piece on after dipping it. Finally, open the jars of paint you've chosen.

I

## Creating designs with the paint

**2.** Use cotton swabs or craft sticks to drop drops of different colors on the surface of the water to create your own unique design. Because the paint is solvent based, it won't mix with the water but will rest on top of it. You will see that some colors tend to spread out over the water, while others stay in one place. You can have fun with creating completely unique designs by moving the colors around with a craft stick to create a swirly design, for example, or just by superimposing the colors on top of each other. There are tons of possibilities!

For an interesting result, cover the surface of the water entirely with paint. If you don't like your result, simply scrape away all the colors with a craft stick (instead of dipping your piece in) and start over again.

**3.** As soon as you're satisfied with your mixture of colors, go on to the next step.

2

2

3

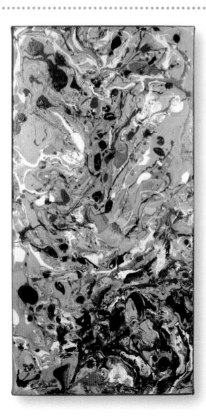

Examples of various colorful designs

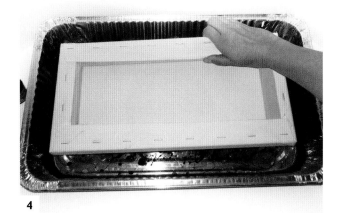

**4**

**5**

A design on canvas

## Dipping the piece

*Wearing rubber gloves for this process is recommended.*

4. As soon as your design is ready, carefully dip your project in the water—but don't immerse it completely. Dip it just enough for the colors to adhere to the piece.

The gloves will prevent staining your hands, as some pieces will require getting your fingers in the water. Once the paint has been transferred to the piece, feel free to admire your result.

If you aren't satisfied, or you want to add more colors, add paint to a batch of fresh water and dip the piece again. Both coats of paint will be visible, giving a unique result. You can add several layers of paint in this way, one on top of another, until you get the look you want.

Note, however, that you can't go back and *remove* colors unless you clean the piece completely with solvent—and this option isn't very pleasant to do.

5. Once the project is finished, clean up any drips and let the project dry completely, laid flat, for about 24 hours.

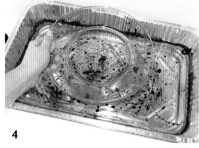

**4**

Dipping a glass plate

**5**

The result

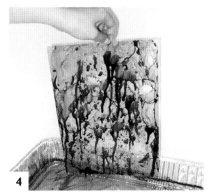

**4**

A rectangle of plexiglass

**5**

The result

## Important

This technique is best for painting objects that are for decoration only. For example, you can decorate the back of a clear glass plate—the side that does not come in contact with food—but you'll need to wash it by hand, without immersing it in water.

You should not put food on a dish decorated with this technique because the paint can be toxic. The dish will be purely decorative.

This technique only works with solvent-based paint. It does not work with paint that must be cured in an oven, or with water-based paints, such as acrylics.

## 23

Stained-glass greeting cards

## Materials

**Patterns:** Pages 162 and 163
**Surface:** Clear acetate sheets

**Colors used:**
See the color key for each card

**Other products:**
Relief outliner: vermeil gold or color of your choice

**Other materials:**
Card with a window in the front (for a photo)
Scissors
Adhesive paper
Lead pencil
Tracing paper and stylus
Small containers

**Stained-glass cards make great personalized greetings!**

**Simply paint a design on a sheet of acetate and, once it's dry, insert it into the window of a scrapbooking-style photo greeting card.**

**Here are the basic steps for making your own stained-glass card, followed by the color key for each card shown here.**

Merry Christmas!

Merry Christmas!

Happy Birthday!

Happy Birthday!

Happy
Valentine's day!

Happy
Mother's day!

Happy Birthday!

## Preparing the design

**1.** Trace the outline of the window in your card on a piece of tracing paper with a regular lead pencil (as shown). This outline will determine the dimensions of your design.

**2.** Place the design you want to use under this piece of tracing paper and trace it with the pencil.

You can use the designs in this book as inspiration or create your own design. For example, you could use a single design in the center of the frame, or combine several elements in the same card. It's up to you to choose whatever design you like most.

**3.** Once your design is traced, draw a dashed guide line all the way around the design, about half an inch from the frame, to indicate where to cut the excess acetate in the finishing steps.

**4.** Finally, place a square of acetate on top of this design and secure it with masking tape (you can remove the pattern at this point). Wipe off the surface with a clean cloth or paper towel to remove any dust.

## Outlining the design

**5.** Cover all the lines of the design except the frame with the relief outliner. You can wipe up any excess or mistakes as long as the outliner is still wet. In the examples shown here, the text was not outlined with the relief outliner, but you can do so if you like. Let the outliner dry completely.

The lines made by the relief outliner will be very visible. It's extremely important to work carefully when doing this step.

**Variation:** For the card with the flower motif, the little plastic crystals were added at this point. Just fill the centers of the flowers with relief outliner and place the crystals on them while the paint is still fresh. Use pliers to place them and press them down without getting any paint on them.

## Painting

*All the cards are described individually following the general instructions (see the color keys).*

**6.** Paint the different sections of the design. Before you start, tape the acetate securely to the work surface (with the design underneath, if necessary) to keep it from warping while you paint. The surface you are working on should be as light in color as possible so that you can see the colors well.

Use toothpicks to fill in the small sections of the design and a paintbrush for larger ones. If you get paint on the relief outliner, wipe it up quickly, before it dries. Once the sections are all filled in, let dry for 24 hours before going on to the final steps.

**6**

Filling in the design with a toothpick

### Important painting note:

When you paint a stripe of color, don't forget to go past the edge of the frame (about half an inch) so the edge of the stripe isn't visible in the finished card.

### Adding messages

There are several ways to add text to your card: You can stick stickers on the acetate, write the text on a piece of light-colored cardstock and glue it on, write on or under the acetate with permanent marker, or type the text up on the computer and print it on a piece of paper that you can slide underneath the acetate.

### Finishing touches

Once your design is completely dry (after 24 hours), you can assemble your card.

**7.** Cut off the excess acetate around the painted motif.

**8.** Use single- or double-sided tape to attach the motif inside the window of the card, making sure to tape only the outside edge of the acetate—you don't want the tape to be visible through the window.

Note: It is important that the background of your card be the lightest color possible (white is best) so that you can see the colors well. If your card is too dark, tape or glue a piece of white cardstock behind your design.

### Tip

Make your greeting cards several days in advance so the paint smell has time to dissipate.

**7**

Pattern p. 162

Pattern p. 162

Pattern p. 162

# Color keys for stained-glass cards

## Chocolate cupcake

*Crimson, brown, sky blue, orange, lemon, glitter medium, lightening medium*

### Procedure to follow

**Cherry:** Blend of half crimson and half glitter medium
**Three layers of icing:** Blend of half brown and half glitter medium
**Base of cake:** Blend of half sky blue and half glitter medium
**Bottom stripe:** Use a paintbrush to apply a uniform coat of orange paint and add a few drops of lightening medium side by side on the paint. The edge of the stripe can be wavy or straight.
**Dots in background:** lemon (applied with stylus)

## Lime cupcake

*Apple green, crimson, yellow, lemon, sky blue, glitter medium, lightening medium*

### Procedure to follow

**Cherry:** Crimson
**Three layers of icing:** Blend of half apple green and half glitter medium
**Base of cake:** Blend of half yellow and half glitter medium
**Top and bottom stripes:** Use a paintbrush to apply a uniform coat of lemon, then add a few drops of lightening medium side by side on the paint. The edges of the stripes can be wavy or straight.
**Dots in background:** Sky blue (applied with stylus)
**Dots on bottom stripe:** Crimson (applied with stylus)

## Multicolored cupcake

*Crimson, apple green, lemon, sky blue, yellow, glitter medium, lightening medium*

### Procedure to follow

**Cherry:** Crimson
**Icing layer 1:** Blend of half apple green and half glitter medium
**Icing layer 2:** Lemon
**Icing layer 3:** Blend of half sky blue and half glitter medium
**Base of cake:** Fill in with yellow, then add three drops of lightening medium into the paint.
**Bottom stripe:** Use a paintbrush to apply a uniform coat of lemon, then add a few drops of lightening medium side by side on the paint. The edge of the stripe can be wavy or straight.
**Dots above the bottom stripe:** Crimson

Pattern p. 162

## Smiling cupcake

*Turquoise blue, lemon, crimson, apple green, yellow, parma, glitter medium*

### Procedure to follow

**Flame:** Yellow
**Candle:** Lemon
**Icing layer 1:** Blend of half parma and half glitter medium
**Icing layer 2:** Blend of half yellow and half glitter medium
**Icing layer 3:** Blend of half turquoise blue and half glitter medium
**Icing layer 4:** Blend of half apple green and half glitter medium
**Icing layer 5:** Blend of half crimson and half glitter medium
**Base of cake:** Lemon
**Dots in background:** Turquoise blue

Pattern p. 162

## Blue cotton candy

*Sky blue, lemon, crimson, glitter medium*

### Procedure to follow

**Cotton candy:** Blend of half sky blue and half glitter medium
**Cone:** Lemon
**Dots in background:** Crimson, sky blue, lemon, and glitter medium

Pattern p. 162

## Lollipop

*Lemon, old pink, orange, turquoise blue, glitter medium*

### Procedure to follow

**Stick:** Turquoise blue
**Dots in background:** Lemon and old pink
**Lollipop:** Alternate between lemon and orange, gently blending the transitions between colors with a toothpick. Drop little drops of glitter medium over the whole section.

Pattern p. 163

Pattern p. 163

Pattern p. 163

## Rose

*Apple green, lemon, old pink, glitter medium*

### Procedure to follow

**Leaves:** Apple green
**Rose:** Blend of half old pink and half glitter medium
**Bottom stripe:** Use a paintbrush to apply a uniform coat of lemon. The edge of the stripe can be wavy or straight. *Here the white cardstock underneath the acetate was replaced with a piece of silvery textured paper (see the instructions for assembling the card).*

## Heart-shaped balloon

*Apple green, crimson, glitter medium*

### Procedure to follow

**Heart:** Crimson
**Little hearts in background:** Apple green
**Dots in background:** Glitter medium
**Bottom stripe:** Use a paintbrush to apply a uniform coat of glitter medium. The edge of the stripe can be wavy or straight.

## Purple and red Christmas tree ball

*Parma, crimson, gold, glitter medium*

### Procedure to follow

**Metal hanger:** Gold
**Three purple sections:** Blend of half parma and half glitter medium
**Three red sections:** Fill in with crimson, then drop a few drops of glitter medium side by side along the section. Don't blend the glitter medium in; the drops should stay round.
**Dots in background:** glitter medium
**Bottom stripe:** Use a paintbrush to apply a uniform coat of glitter medium. The edge of the stripe can be wavy or straight.
*Here the white cardstock underneath the acetate was replaced with a piece of silvery textured paper (see the instructions for assembling the card).*

Pattern p. 163

Pattern p. 162

Pattern p. 163

## Green and red Christmas tree ball

*Apple green, crimson, gold, glitter medium*

### Procedure to follow

**Metal hanger:** Gold
**Two red sections:** Crimson
**Three green sections:** Fill in with apple green, then add a few drops of glitter medium side by side along the section. Don't blend the glitter medium in; the drops should stay round.
**Dots in background:** Glitter medium
**Bottom stripe:** Blend of half crimson and half glitter medium. Use a paintbrush to apply a uniform coat of the blend along the bottom of the frame. The edge of the stripe can be wavy or straight.

## Candle

*Lemon, sky blue, apple green, crimson, glitter medium*

### Procedure to follow

**Flame:** Lemon
**Candle:** Alternating stripes of crimson and apple green
**Glow around flame:** Glitter medium
**Bottom stripe:** Use a paintbrush to apply a uniform coat of sky blue, then add a few drops of glitter medium side by side on the paint. The edge of the stripe can be wavy or straight.
**Dots in background:** Lemon

## Pretty flowers

*Cobalt blue, crimson, yellow, glitter medium plastic crystals*

### Procedure to follow

**Center flower:** Cobalt blue
**Flower on left:** Crimson
**Flower on right:** Yellow
**Dots in background:** Glitter medium

## 24

*Color me bold!*

This pretty chest of drawers is decorated with a combination of glass paints and acrylics. It's included in this book to show you how you can combine many different products in the same project.

## Materials

**Patterns:** Pages 164 to 167
**Surface:** Unfinished wooden dresser with three drawers
**Measurements:** 24 x 28 x 12 in.

**Glass paint colors used:**
White, sky blue, lemon, parma, salmon, apple green, old pink

**Acrylic paint colors used:**
Bright orange, carousel pink, calypso blue, sour apple, lavender, black plum

**Other products:**
Relief outliner: black
Glitter medium
Gloss gel medium (embossed effect)
Matte or gloss varnish (your choice)
Gesso

**Other materials:**
Sandpaper (optional)
Ruler and lead pencil
Black carbon paper and stylus
Synthetic flat paintbrushes (different sizes for painting different sections)
Foam stamps (design of your choice)
Natural-bristle brush for the glass paint

## Preparing the dresser and applying the base colors

1. Remove the knobs from the drawers and sand the dresser if necessary so it is smooth and soft to the touch.

2. Use a flat paintbrush to apply two coats of gesso over the whole dresser. This will completely hide the grain of the wood and yield brighter colors. Let dry.

3. Next, use flat paintbrushes to paint each part of the dresser, with two coats, if needed.

**First drawer:** Calypso blue
**Second drawer:** Carousel pink
**Third drawer:** Sour apple
**Top and bottom of the dresser:** Bright orange
**Sides of the dresser:** Lavender
**Knobs (six in all):** Two bright orange, two sour apple, and two calypso blue

3

## Transferring the patterns

4. Use the stylus and carbon paper to transfer the patterns onto the dresser as follows:

**Three drawers:** Use the stylus and carbon paper to transfer the pattern (flowers and curve) onto each drawer (centered).
**Top of dresser:** Transfer only the curve pattern without the flowers.
**Sides of dresser:** Transfer the large flower pattern onto each side of the dresser, about one-third of the way

Pattern: flowers and curve

down. Use a pencil to draw a long stem with loops that goes down to the bottom of the side. (See photo on p. 126)

Pattern: large flower

## Background coat on the flowers

5. Use a flat brush to apply two coats of gesso over all the flowers. Let dry.

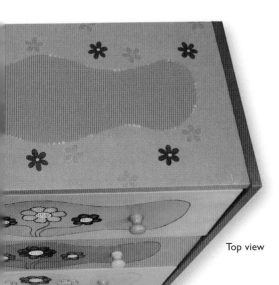

Top view

5

5

## Outlining the design

**6.** Cover all the outlines of the flowers, stems, and large curves—except the one on the top of the dresser—with the black relief outliner. You can correct any mistakes by wiping the paint off quickly with a clean, damp cotton swab. Let dry for 30 minutes.

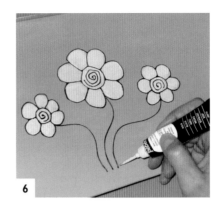

## Color key (base colors)

**First drawer (blue)**
**Central flower:** Lemon
**Two small flowers:** Old pink
**Centers of flowers:** White

**Second drawer (pink)**
**Central flower:** Parma
**Two small flowers:** Salmon
**Centers of flowers:** White

**Third drawer (green)**
**Central flower:** Sky blue
**Two small flowers:** Lemon
**Centers of flowers:** White
**Large flower on left side:** Apple green
**Center:** Old pink
**Large flower on right side:** Old pink
**Center:** Apple green

## Painting the flowers

You must work with the surface flat and level, since the glass paint is very fluid. Lay the dresser down on its side and paint one side at a time. When you have finished painting all the flowers, let them dry completely before moving on to the next step.

Here is the technique for each of the flowers. Paint them one at a time.

**7.** Fill in all the petals of one flower with the base color indicated (see the color key). Use plenty of paint to obtain a shiny, even look.

**8.** Use a cotton swab to drop one or several drops of glitter medium on each petal. Have fun with creating different and original designs in each flower. Let dry as is.

Note: For the flowers on the sides of the dresser, do the petals one at a time, since these sections are very large and take longer to fill in.

The center of each flower is simply filled in with the color indicated without any special effects.

Left side

Right side

## Adding texture and color to the curves

**9.** Use gloss gel medium to create the embossed effect on the inside of each large curved shape—except for on the flowers. Let dry for several hours until the gel becomes completely clear.

**10.** Use a paintbrush to spread a thin coat of lemon glass paint over the textured section. Let dry again for 24 hours.

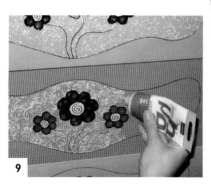

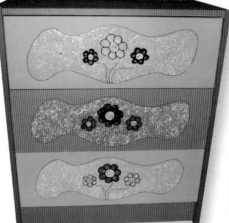

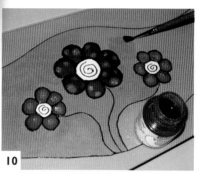

## Finishing touches

*Top of dresser*

**11.** Paint the section inside the curve with carousel pink (two coats, using a flat paintbrush) and let dry.

**12.** Apply a thin coat of calypso blue paint to the flower-shaped stamp and stamp this design several times on the top of the dresser.

**13.** Add more paint to the stamp after every impression to obtain a uniform effect. Add several stamped designs to the sides of the dresser.

**14.** Repeat with a second stamp and the black plum paint.

*Decorative dots*

**15.** Dip the handle of your paintbrush in the sour apple paint and use it to create sets of four dots along the edge of the curved shape, with several sets scattered all the way around. Let dry.

*Varnish*

**16.** Varnish the dresser and the knobs—except for the sections painted with glass paint—to protect the paint.

12

Cupcake (canvas version)

## Materials

**Pattern:** Page 168
**Surface:** Artist's canvas
**Measurements:** 6 x 6 in.,
or the size of your choice

**Colors used:**
Sky blue, sun yellow, wheat
yellow, white, clementine,
lemon, red

**Other products:**
Relief outliner: black
Lightening medium
Glitter medium
Gesso and a flat paintbrush
Bright red acrylic paint

**Other materials:**
Small container
Black carbon paper and
    stylus
Eraser

## Preparing the piece

**1.** Use the flat paintbrush to apply a coat of gesso over the whole surface. Let dry.

## Transferring the pattern

**2.** Next, place the pattern on the canvas and attach it at the top with tape.

**3.** Insert a piece of carbon paper underneath the pattern with the dark side down and use the stylus to transfer the design to the surface.

## Outlining the design

**4.** Go over all the lines of the design (except the outside edge) with the relief outliner. Let dry. Erase any graphite lines still visible.

## Painting

**5.** Fill in the following sections with the colors indicated. Use toothpicks for the small sections and a paintbrush for the larger ones.

**A:** Red (paintbrush or toothpick)
**B:** Sun yellow (paintbrush)
**C:** Clementine (paintbrush)

Sections D, E, and F are different and are described at right.

Once the project is painted, let it dry for 24 hours before going on to the last step.

### Section D

*Blend of half sky blue and half glitter medium*

**6.** Paint the section with the blend, then use a cotton swab to add a few drops of glitter medium of different sizes over the whole section. Let dry as is.

### E sections

*Wheat yellow and white*

**7.** Alternate between wheat yellow and white for the sections of the cupcake paper.

### Section F (background)

*Lemon and glitter medium*

The background of the canvas is painted in three steps. Don't let it dry in between steps.

**8.** Start by applying a coat of lemon over the whole background, to about a quarter inch from the edge of the canvas.

**9.** As soon as the background is covered with paint, use a clean cotton swab to remove the paint around the edge of the central motif, leaving a lighter outline. Use as many cotton swabs as necessary, as they will fill up with paint quickly.

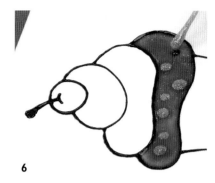

6

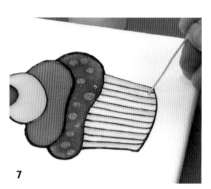

7

8

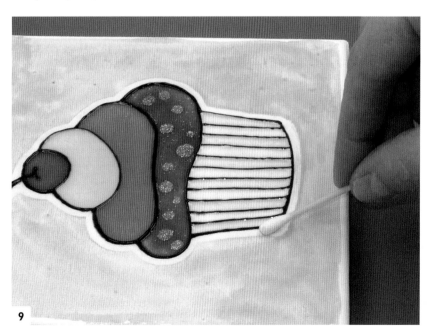

9

**10.** Lastly, add several drops of lightening medium all over the background to give it some dimension, varying the size of the drops. Let dry.

### Finishing touches

Finish with the following details:

### Section B

**11.** Add little lines of relief outliner (about a quarter inch), going in all directions, throughout the section.

### Section C

**12.** Dip the end of the paintbrush handle in the red paint and use it to add dots throughout the section.

### Edge and sides of the canvas

**13.** Use the flat paintbrush to paint the unpainted border of the canvas as well as the sides with the bright red acrylic paint of your choice. Let dry.

**14.** Dip a stylus in the red glass paint and use it to add little dots all the way around the edge of the border between the two colors for a nice finishing touch. Let the project dry for 24 hours.

10

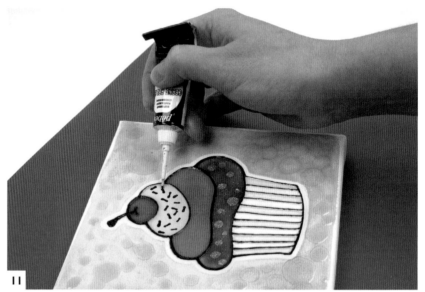

11

12

# Appendices

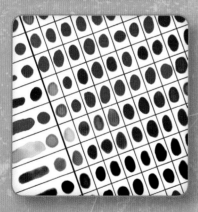

**Charts of colors and blends**
- Vitrail (Pébéo) product line
- Chart of transparent colors
- Chart of opaque colors
- Chart of flesh tones

**Common problems and questions**

# Charts of colors and blends

The information contained in this chapter is included for information purposes only. It is certainly possible that, over time, some products may no longer be available or certain colors or numbers may change.

**Vitrail (Pébéo) product line**

## Transparent colors

| List of colors | Number | English name |
|---|---|---|
| Blanc | 20 | White |
| Bleu ciel | 36 | Sky blue |
| Bleu cobalt | 37 | Cobalt blue |
| Bleu profond | 10 | Deep blue |
| Bleu turquoise | 17 | Turquoise blue |
| Brun | 11 | Brown |
| Chartreuse | 18 | Chartreuse |
| Citron | 23 | Lemon |
| Cramoisi | 12 | Crimson |
| Émeraude | 13 | Emerald |
| Greengold | 22 | Greengold |
| Jaune | 14 | Yellow |
| Nacré | 39 | Pearl |
| Noir | 15 | Black |
| Or | 38 | Gold |
| Orange | 16 | Orange |
| Parme | 33 | Parma |
| Pourpre | 26 | Purple |
| Rose | 21 | Pink |
| Sable | 30 | Sand |
| Saumon | 32 | Salmon |
| Vert foncé | 35 | Dark green |
| Vert pomme | 34 | Apple Green |
| Vieux rose | 31 | Old pink |
| Violet | 25 | Violet |
| Violet rouge | 19 | Red Violet |

## Opaque colors

| List of colors | Number | English name |
|---|---|---|
| Bleu jeans | 44 | Blue jeans |
| Bleu océan | 43 | Ocean blue |
| Clémentine | 46 | Clementine |
| Étain | 47 | Pewter |
| Jaune blé | 40 | Wheat yellow |
| Jaune soleil | 41 | Sun yellow |
| Or chaud | 48 | Warm gold |
| Rouge | 45 | Red |
| Super blanc | 49 | Super white |
| Vert clair | 42 | Light green |

## Other products in the Vitrail line

| French name | English name |
|---|---|
| Médium éclaircissant | Lightening medium |
| Médium pailleté | Glitter medium |
| Médium mat | Matte medium |
| Médium à craqueler | Crackle medium |

# Chart of transparent colors

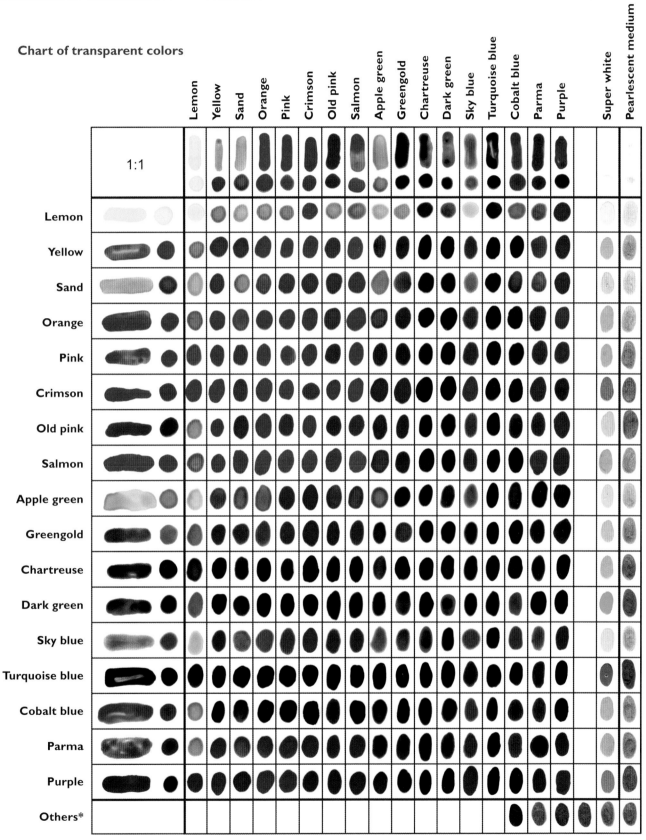

* Note that there are other colors (in the chart on the previous page) that are not included in this table, because they are too dark to show up well. However, you can see the color well when mixed with Pearlescent medium (Black, Brown, Violet, Deep blue, Dark green, Red violet).

# Chart of opaque colors

| 1:1 | Wheat yellow | Sun yellow | Clementine | Red | Light green | Ocean blue | Blue jeans | Super white | Pearlescent medium |
|---|---|---|---|---|---|---|---|---|---|
| **Wheat yellow** | | | | | | | | | |
| **Sun yellow** | | | | | | | | | |
| **Clementine** | | | | | | | | | |
| **Red** | | | | | | | | | |
| **Light green** | | | | | | | | | |
| **Ocean blue** | | | | | | | | | |
| **Blue jeans** | | | | | | | | | |
| **Super white** | | | | | | | | | |
| **Pearlescent medium** | | | | | | | | | |

\* Note that the colors Pewter and Warm gold are not included in this table

# Chart of flesh tones

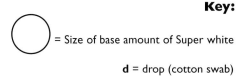

= Size of base amount of Super white

**d** = drop (cotton swab)

**Result**          **Blend**

| | | |
|---|---|---|
| A = | | A = Super white + 1 d Pink |
| B = | | B = Super white + 2 d Pink + 2 d Lemon |
| C = | | C = Super white + 1 d Salmon |
| D = | | D = Super white + 1 d Red (small) |
| E = | | E = Super white + 4 d Wheat yellow + 1 d Red |
| F = | | F = Super white + 3 d Wheat yellow + 2 d Red |
| G = | | G = Super white + 1 d Crimson + 1 d Yellow |
| H = | | H = Superwhite + 1 d Crimson + 1 d Lemon |

The method for creating a "flesh tone" blend is the same for each of the recipes in the table above.

Always start by putting the base color (Super white) in the container. Next, add several drops of the color(s) indicated in the recipe and mix it all together. Make a small test batch before mixing up a larger blend.

Adding a "drop" consists of dipping a clean cotton swab in the paint and adding a small drop of the paint into the blend. Mix the blend every time you add a drop of paint to check the tint obtained.

Remember: Add the drops one at a time, or add half drops as needed, to control the intensity of the color. One drop too many, or one too-large drop, and you'll immediately find yourself with a "jaundiced" skin tone or a dark pink. If this happens, you'll need to add more white to the blend to create a paler tone.

If bubbles form in the paint, let it sit for a while before using it.

# Common problems and questions

### The relief outliner isn't coming out of the tube.

The tip is probably blocked. Unscrew it and clean it with warm, soapy water until it is completely clean. Use a needle to remove the blockage if needed.

The problem could also be that the protective film isn't completely broken. If this is the case, remove it completely.

### The relief outliner is coming out of the other end of the tube.

Make sure the protective film is completely removed and the tip isn't blocked.

### The adhesive lead strip isn't sticking.

If the lead strips don't stick well, they've probably been manipulated too much—pressed down, pulled up, reattached, pressed down again. Or the surface may not be completely clean, or there may be a fingerprint in the spot where the strip isn't sticking.

### There are bubbles in the paint.

See what happens when you put the paint in a section of the design. Are there still bubbles? If so, the jar was mixed too much. Let it sit for several minutes. If, on the contrary, there aren't any, but the bubbles appear when you apply the paint gradually, the problem is probably that you are patting the paint too much with the brush, or that the brush is ragged. Try a different brush to see if you get the same result. You can pop the larger bubbles with a needle before they dry.

### Where can I get plexiglass to paint on?

At any glass or home improvement store. Plexiglass is available in several thicknesses, and, as a general rule, the thicker it is, the better it will keep its shape. The price varies with the size and desired thickness. A nice things about using plexiglass is that you can make holes in the ends to hang the piece with chains, and thus hang it without using a frame. (Remember to make the holes before painting the section.)

### Where can I find other patterns for stained glass painting?

The pattern packets collection Julie's Crafting Ideas contains several titles on the subject of stained glass painting. The projects in these books include step-by-step photos and instructions from start to finish, allowing you to learn all sorts of different techniques. There is also a DVD of techniques for those who would like to learn even more: *Faux-Vitrail Techniques*. Visit www.juliescraftingideas.com for more information.

### Can I add a second coat of paint once the first coat is dry?

Yes, you can add a second coat of paint, but doing so might cause the paints to react—little cracks will appear. Often, there is no reaction, but it's important to be aware of the possibility, because it can happen. If you add a second coat, do it over the whole section. Otherwise, there will be a line at the edge of the new coat. Sometimes a second coat will be necessary with certain colors that can become discolored over time.

### Can I add solvent to paint that has become thick?

If the paint in the jar gets too thick, there is unfortunately not much you can do. For paint that is slightly thick, I recommend adding a small amount of odorless mineral spirits to the thickened paint to give it some fluidity. You can also add lightening medium to the paint, which will also make the paint more transparent.

### Can I dry the acrylic gel medium with a hair dryer to speed up the drying?

I don't recommended speeding up the drying process with a hair dryer when you are working on a stained glass painting project. The reason is very simple: The hair dryer quickly forms a crust on the medium, which prevents it drying all the way through. The result is that the texture stays white even after hours of drying. One solution, if this happens, is to pierce the white sections with a needle to allow a little air in. If this doesn't work, the only alternative is to scrape off the medium with a craft knife and start again.

When you apply gel medium, make sure you aren't putting it on too thick, even when creating an embossed effect. One or two hours at most should be sufficient for it to become completely clear.

If you are layering textures on top of each other, make sure the first coat is completely dry and clear before going on with the second one. This way, you won't have any problems with drying.

### The gel medium is still white even when completely dry.

Check the label of your product—some mediums have a matte finish. If it is definitely supposed to dry clear, but it stays white, it's probably a manufacturing flaw.

### Can you remove paint from the relief outliner once everything is dry?

You must remove any paint that gets on the relief outliner while it is still wet, using a cotton swab. If the paint is dry, it is, unfortunately, impossible to remove. You can, however, retouch problem sections with a fine paintbrush and the appropriate color of paint, or go over the outline of the section again.

If the paint has begun to dry and is sticky to the touch, dip a cotton swab in solvent and blot off the excess on a paper towel. Gently rub the relief outliner to remove the paint from it.

### How can I correct a defect in a stained glass painting—visible blob of gel medium or uneven paint?

You can add a very thin coat of paint in the problem section. The color will be darker, but that will make the flaw less obvious.

### Can I put adhesive lead strips on canvas?

Yes, you can, but you must put a flat object (such as a book) underneath the canvas to support it while you press the lead strips down. I would apply a coat of gesso over the canvas first to make the surface smoother.

### There are many consistencies of gesso available. Which should I use?

The consistency of the gesso is not important. The goal is to create an opaque white foundation with no visible brushstrokes. Usually this can be done in one or two coats if the gesso is of good quality and the grain of the wood is pale, but it is possible that it will take three or even four coats if you are using a very thin or low-quality product.

### The Vitrail product line has two other mediums (matte medium and crackle medium) that aren't mentioned in this book. Where can I learn more about using these products?

The uses of these mediums are described in the DVD *Faux-Vitrail Techniques*.

### Can I store the jars of paint in an unheated garage?

The products used in this book (paints, mediums, gesso, and so on) should not be frozen. Keep them in a dry place with a consistent temperature, not exposed to light.

Vitrail products and gloss gel medium in a tube:
Pébéo
www.pebeo.com

Framed glass panes: Gotrick, Inc.
www.gotrickinc.com

Tea caddy and wooden base for block of glass:
Marc Drainville, Artisan
www.marcdrainville.com

Wooden tortoise and hollow glass block:
Biblairie GGC, Sherbrooke, Quebec
www.biblairie.qc.ca

Wardrobe door and dresser: Ikea
www.ikea.com

Various painting materials:
www.deserres.ca

See also the list of stores on:
www.juliescraftingideas.com

Peel off stickers:
www.starform.com

Must-see site for information and publications
on decorative arts:
www.diffuzart.com

Stencils for stained glass painting and stained glass greeting
cards: "Des idées plein la tête" collection
www.juliescraftingideas.com

To learn more about Julie Lafaille:
www.juliescraftingideas.com
Email: julielafaille@juliescraftingideas.com
Facebook group

# Patterns

This chapter contains all the patterns needed to make the projects in this book. Some patterns will need to be enlarged on a photocopier in order to make the projects in their original sizes.

Don't hesitate to change the suggested sizes in order to adapt a piece to your decor. For example, a project on a small canvas measuring 5 by 5 inches can be enlarged for a canvas measuring 15 by 15 inches by enlarging the pattern 300 percent.

*1. Sparkling rose*

For original size, enlarge this pattern to 125%

central section

**Source:** Julie Lafaille, *Stained Glass Painting,* Stackpole Books 2015

2. *Art deco tulips*

For original size, enlarge this pattern to 125%

*3. Favorite frame*

For original size, use this pattern at 100%

**Source:** Julie Lafaille, *Stained Glass Painting*, Stackpole Books 2015

4. *A flower for you*

For original size, use this pattern at 100%

*5. Cupcake (relief outliner version)*

For original size, use this pattern at 100%

R

O

O

R

J

J

C

M1

M2

R

V

R

O

O

R

**Source:** Julie Lafaille, *Stained Glass Painting*, Stackpole Books 2015

*6. Cupcake (lead strip version)*

For original size, use this pattern at 100%

| C | | | | C |

V · J · J · V

V · O · O · V

V · V

J · O · O · J

central section
(sticker)

J · O · C · J

V · V

V · O · O · V

V · J · J · V

| C | | | | C |

**Source:** Julie Lafaille, *Stained Glass Painting*, Stackpole Books 2015

*7. Stained glass with sticker*                    For original size, enlarge this pattern to 150%

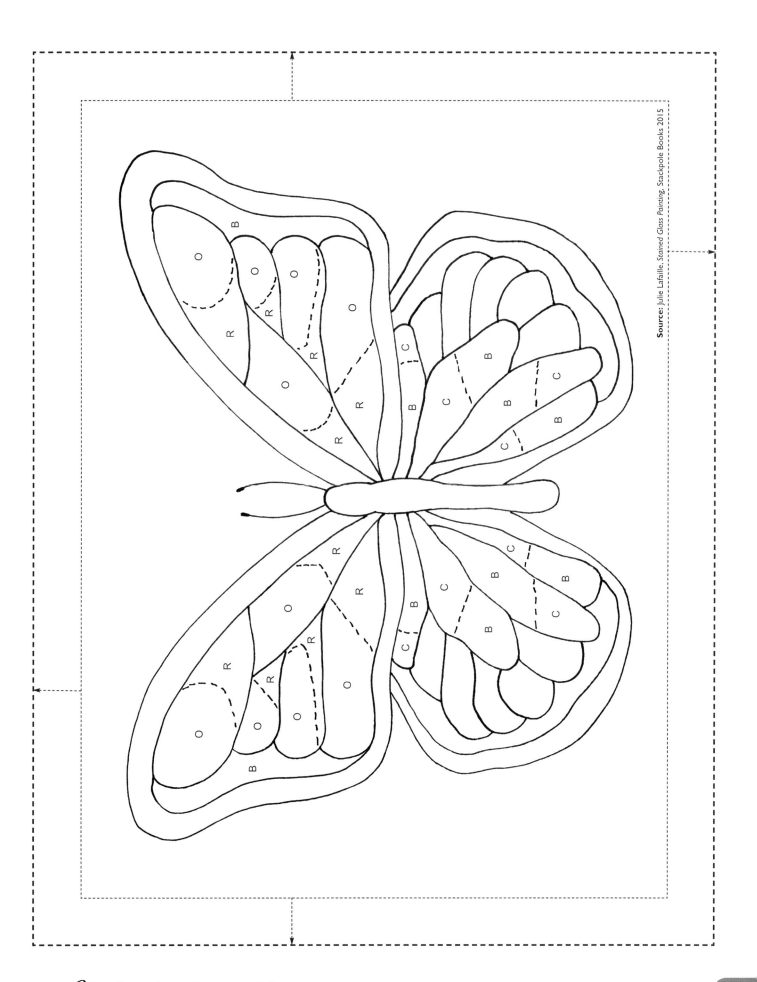

8. *Multicolored butterfly*

For original size, enlarge this pattern to 150%

*9. Lighted glass block*

For original size, use this pattern at 100%

**Source:** Julie Lafaille, *Stained Glass Painting*, Stackpole Books 2015

*10. Red tulips*

For original size, enlarge this pattern to 200%

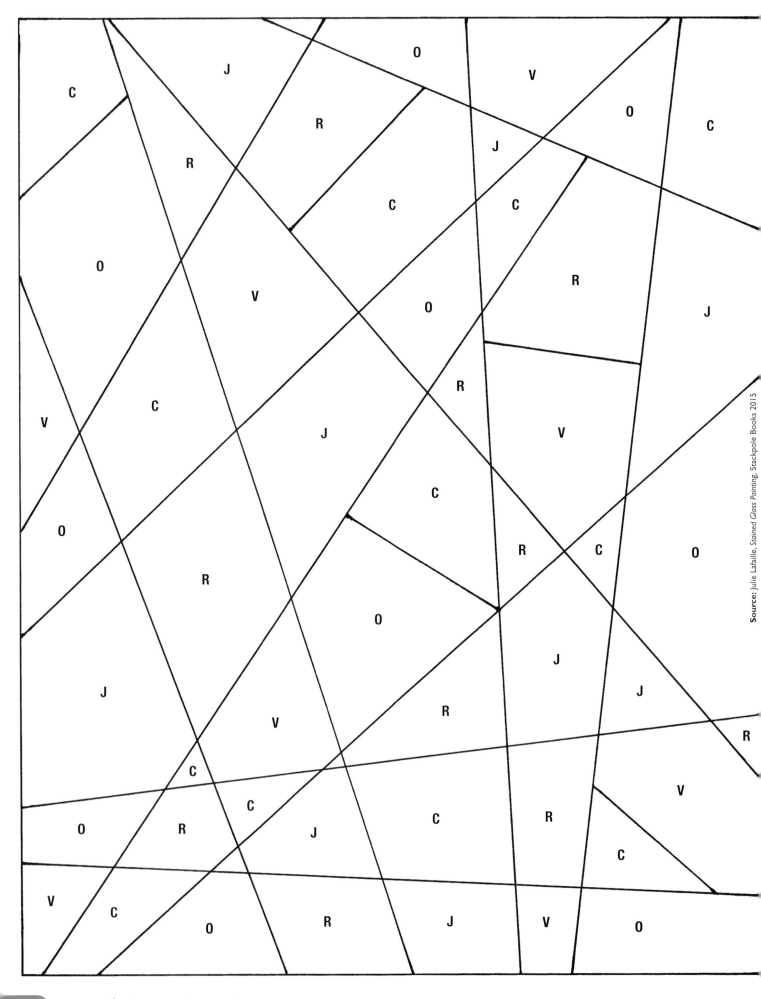

*11. Colored glass tiles*                    For original size, use this pattern at 100%

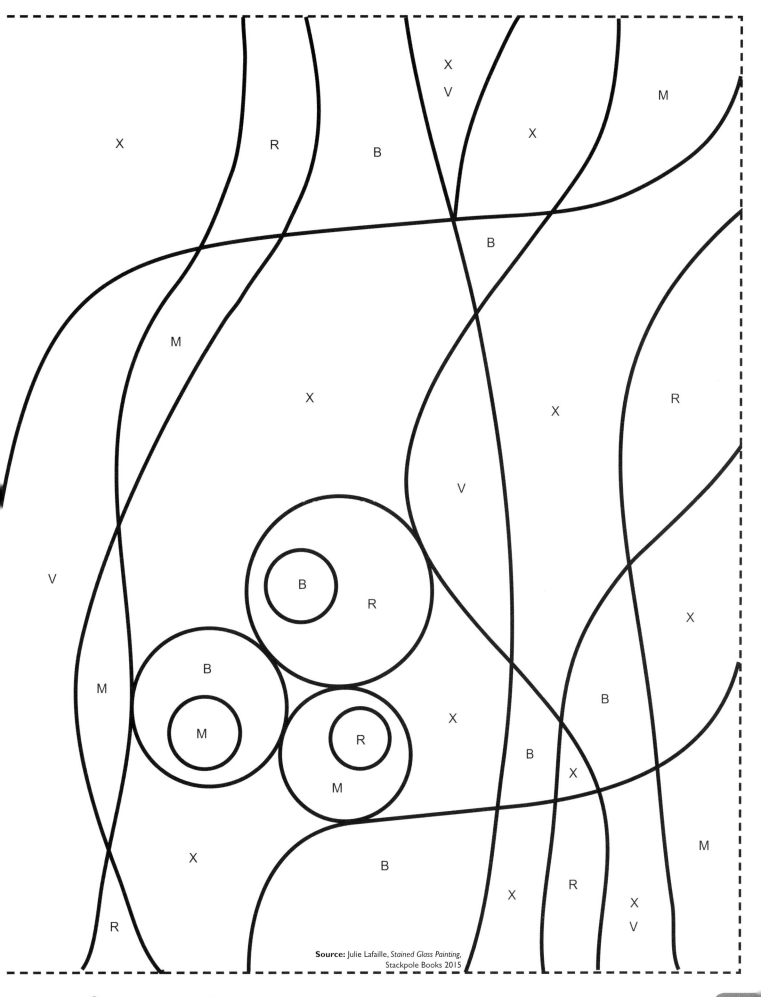

**Source:** Julie Lafaille, *Stained Glass Painting*, Stackpole Books 2015

*12. Art deco panel*

For original size, use this pattern at 100%

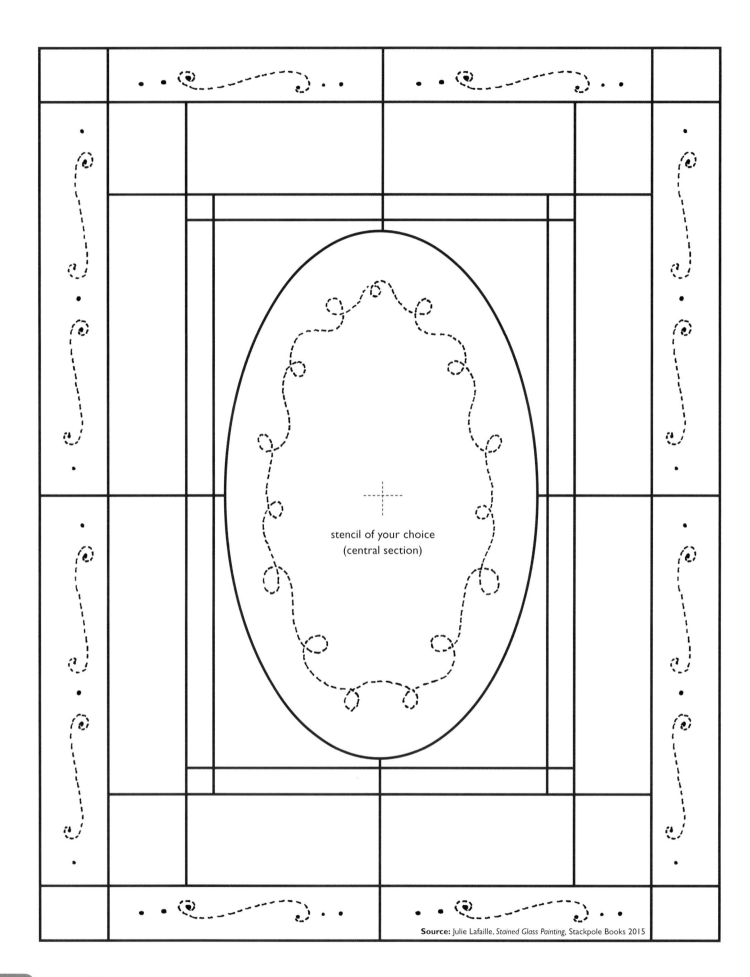

stencil of your choice
(central section)

**Source:** Julie Lafaille, *Stained Glass Painting*, Stackpole Books 2015

*13. Dare to go transparent*

For original size, enlarge this pattern to 150%

Source: Julie Lafaille, *Stained Glass Painting*, Stackpole Books 2015

For original size, use this pattern at 100%

**1**

**2**

**Source:** Julie Lafaille, *Stained Glass Painting*, Stackpole Books 2015

Attach together with the dotted line of part 1 over the dotted line of part 2.

*15. Elongated format*

For original size, enlarge this pattern to 250%

**1**

**2**

Attach together with the dotted line of part 1 over the dotted line of part 2.

*15. Elongated format (mirror image)*

For original size, enlarge this pattern to 250%

*16. Decorative plaque—Bee*     For original size, use this pattern at 100%

Source: Julie Lafaille, *Stained Glass Painting*. Stackpole Books 2015

*17. Decorative plaque—Frog*

Welcome

*18. Decorative plaque—Sunflower*     For original size, use this pattern at 100%

**Source:** Julie Lafaille, *Stained Glass Painting*, Stackpole Books 2015

*19. Elegant mirror*

For original size, enlarge this pattern to 150%

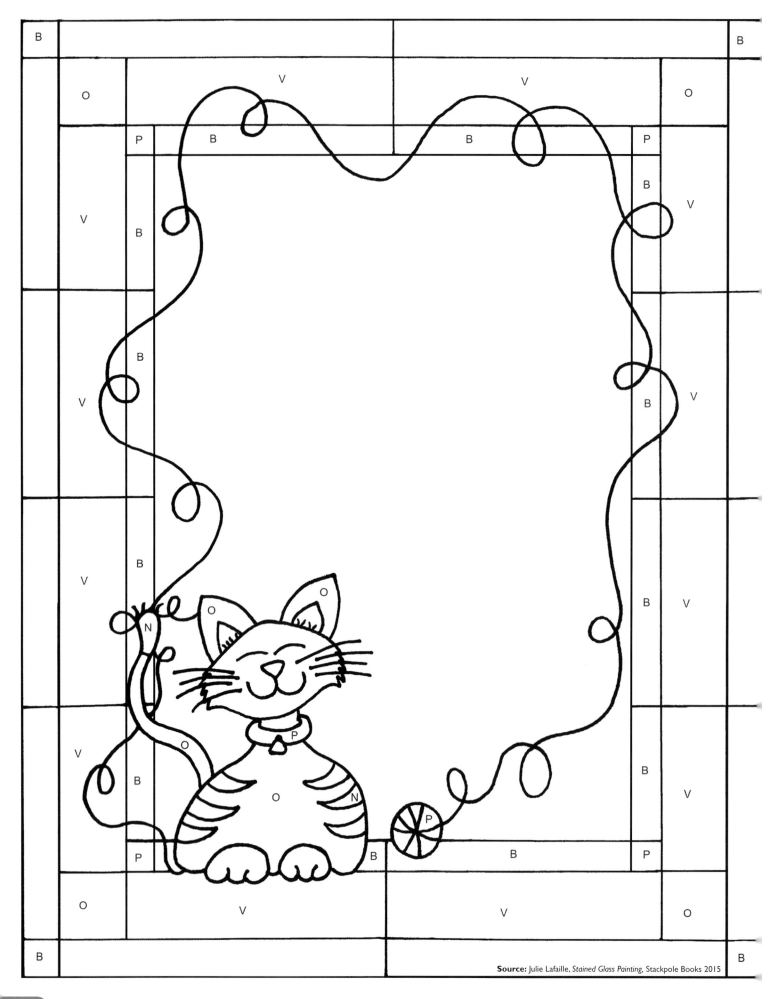

20. *Kitten mirror*

For original size, enlarge this pattern to 200%

Source: Julie Lafaille, *Stained Glass Painting*, Stackpole Books 2015

*21. Peace tortoise*

For original size, use this pattern at 100%

Happy Birthday!

Happy Birthday!

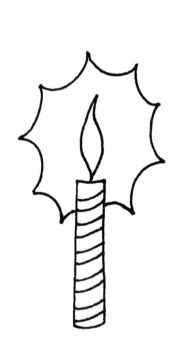

Happy Birthday!

Happy Birthday!

Happy Birthday!

**Source:** Julie Lafaille, *Stained Glass Painting*, Stackpole Books 2015

*23. Stained-glass greeting cards*     For original size, use these patterns at 100%

Merry Christmas!

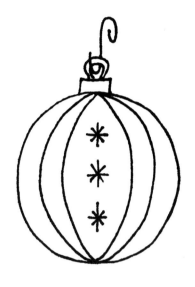

Merry Christmas!

Happy Birthday!

Happy
Mother's day!

Happy
Valentine's day!

**Source:** Julie Lafaille, *Stained Glass Painting*, Stackpole Books 2015

*23. Stained-glass greeting cards*

For original size, use these patterns at 100%

Source: Julie Lafaille, *Stained Glass Painting*, Stackpole Books 2015

Flower for the sides
of the dresser

*24. Color me bold!*

For original size, use this pattern at 100%

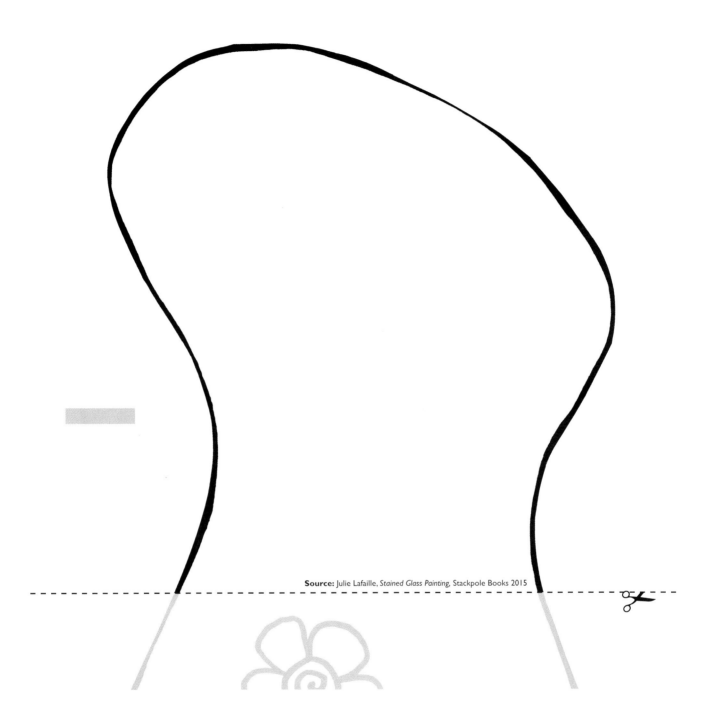

**Source:** Julie Lafaille, *Stained Glass Painting*, Stackpole Books 2015

Attach this pattern to part 2 from the next page.

*24. Color me bold!*

For original size, use this pattern at 100%

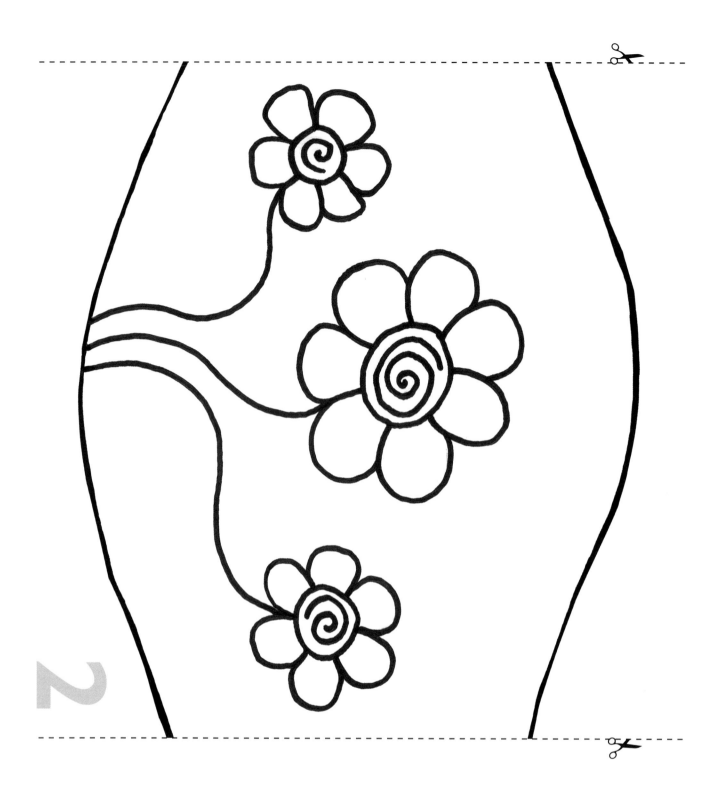

Attach this pattern to part 1 from the previous page and part 3 from the next page.

*24. Color me bold!* For original size, use this pattern at 100%

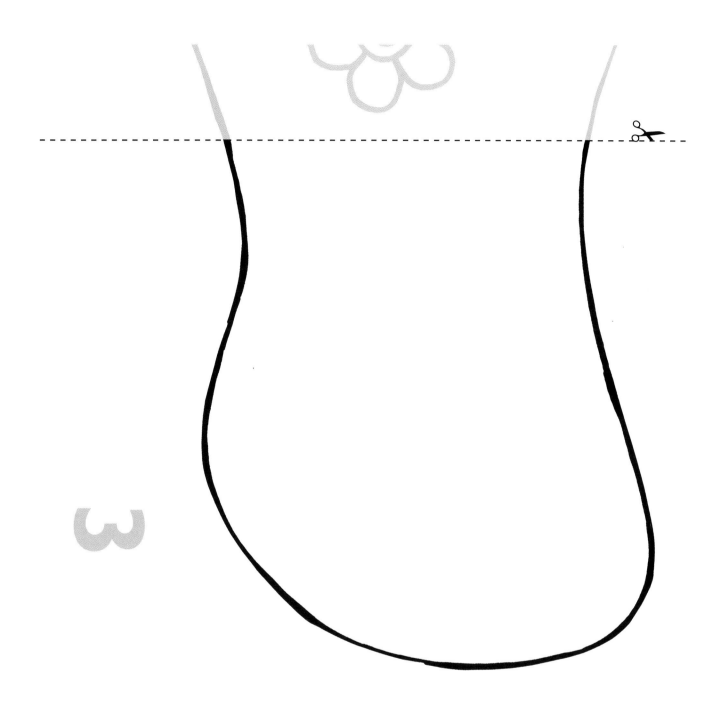

Attach this pattern to part 2 from the previous page.

For original size, use this pattern at 100%

Source: Julie Lafaille, *Stained Glass Painting*, Stackpole Books 2015

25. *Cupcake (canvas version)*

For original size, use this pattern at 100%

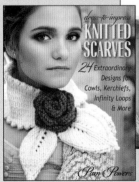